THE CHURCH
IN EXPERIMENT

STUDIES IN NEW
CONGREGATIONAL STRUCTURES
AND FUNCTIONAL MISSION

THE CHURCH IN EXPERIMENT

Rüdiger Reitz

ABINGDON PRESS   Nashville and New York

SET UP, PRINTED, AND BOUND BY THE
PARTHENON PRESS, AT NASHVILLE,
TENNESSEE, UNITED STATES OF AMERICA

To the Christian Theological Seminary, Indianapolis,
because of its ecumenical commitment, and those
who are trying to make a difference in church
and society

FOREWORD

The late Dr. Robert Spike once observed that as a parish pastor in his early ministry he had been aware that the churches were in trouble. When he accepted a denominational mission post that took him around the country, he discovered that the situation was even worse than he had imagined. But at the same time, he said, "I discovered more signs of hope in the churches than I had dared expect." Rüdiger Reitz with the tenacity of a bloodhound has sniffed out these signs of hope and sought to make available to churchmen the insights of the significant experimentation in Christian life and witness that has been developing with increasing momentum since the end of World War II.

To present this wide range of material with order and lucidity has been a very demanding task. In the United States, there have been both the resources and the freedom, in many places, to undertake a great diversity of new ministries that are difficult to put into neat categories or analyze very systematically. In this book we now have a phenomenology of the experimental church which will provide a path for others through the jungle of church renewal. Herein lies the unique contribution of *The Church in Experiment*. It is not simply another rehash of the story of familiar renewal literature landmarks like The Church of the Saviour, East Harlem Protestant Parish, and the

Detroit Industrial Mission. Nor will the reader find primarily a catalogue of present experiments in church renewal and mission. The author makes available to us, with keen critical judgment and careful discernment, what is important and relevant in the experience of each of the situations he discusses and under headings that make this mound of information readily useful. The result is the first systematic study of church experimentation yet produced.

The Church in Experiment in many ways is a volume complementary to *The Church for Others,* the World Council of Churches' study reports on the "missionary structures of the congregation." The fundamental issues in church renewal now center around church structures rather than theological considerations. A generation of young clergy, supported by a broad shelf of books on church renewal and mission theology, have been wrecked on the shoals of morphological fundamentalism, the rigidity of ecclesiastical structures. *The Church for Others* provides a solid foundation in sociological and theological terms for the church in mission. *The Church in Experiment* provides a host of parables in which we take a careful look in each case at the ecclesiology that lies behind the experiment. There is no more urgent task today for the churches than to break the hold of traditional forms and find the structures that enable them to join in God's mission.

One result of the "missionary structures study" in the United States has been the rather bitter argument between those who argue that the normative form of the church is the residential parish or congregation and those who, often writing off the congregation, are searching for new forms of missionary presence in the worlds other than residence that dominate the lives of men today. Rüdiger Reitz simply ignores this sterile argument, and by the ordering of his material makes clear that he believes emphatically in the need for renewal in old forms and the development of new ones. He uses the categories of "congregational structures" and "functional mission," in what provides an effective pattern for organizing his material.

8

FOREWORD

Here is a gold mine of ideas and experience that will be useful to Christians everywhere as they seek to find structures for mission—not in the form of blueprints or directives, but as parables that provide both encouragement and clues that must be pursued and given specificity in one's own context and experimentation.

GEORGE W. WEBBER

ACKNOWLEDGMENTS

The idea for this book originated in one of the numerous conversations I had with Dr. Edwin Becker, professor of Sociology of Religion at Christian Theological Seminary in Indianapolis, Indiana, after the completion of a coast-to-coast "church renewal exploring tour" with my wife in the summer of 1967. I am deeply grateful for his keen interest in my work and his critical assistance during the research for this study. He also arranged for the necessary funds for the second term of the research period.

A special word of acknowledgment is due Dr. James Armstrong, now bishop of The United Methodist Church in the Dakotas and formerly senior minister at Broadway United Methodist Church in Indianapolis. He made me see that in the process of church renewal the supplement to a scientific methodology is a radical commitment to man in his manifold estrangements. He convinced me that a minister today needs to get engaged in the social and political struggles of his community.

I am grateful to Dr. Beauford Norris, President of Christian Theological Seminary, for generously providing the funds for my work, and for his promotion of the ecumenical scholarship idea in the life of the expanding Seminary.

I also owe warmest thanks to Mr. Pierce S. Ellis, college editor of Abingdon Press, in particular, and to the publishing company in general for their readiness to keep the debate on church renewal going by providing a platform for European theologians to make their contribution to efforts made in the U.S.A. that aim at authentic church structures for this time. Mr. Ellis undertook the task of eliminating the "Germanics" and "Englishing" the manuscript. Because of his patience and generosity, preparations for the publication of this book proceeded extraordinarily well, the distance between the U.S.A. and Germany notwithstanding.

Without the assistance of the scholarship committees of the World Council of Churches in Geneva and New York I would not have had the chance to spend two years of academic work in the U.S.A. I would like for this book to contribute to the ecumenical and transatlantic exchange of concepts and models in church reform. Likewise, I wish to prove that ecumenicity today will cease to be mere theory once publications—such as this one—yield increased efforts for the realization of a challenging and more frequent cooperation between Christians in the U.S.A. and Europe.

Finally, I would like to assure friends and all others with whom I discussed or corresponded on matters of church reform that without this sort of communication I would not have been able to deal with church renewal in its complexity and entanglement.

RUDIGER REITZ
Frankfurt (Main), Germany
June 6, 1969

CONTENTS

INTRODUCTION
Signs of Church Renewal

At present American Protestantism is in the process of exercising experimentation as the life style of the church. The period of shy attempts (1945-1955) in which the subsequent criteria were set up for the renewal of American Protestantism has given way to a broad reform movement. Perhaps the term "reform" is now too inadequate to express the enthusiasm and the range of the whole process. If age-old structures of the parish have been pushed aside, if some churches have become something like laboratories for mission, if ministers have tried to surpass each other in worldliness, then revolution has become a fact. An era in American Protestantism has dawned in which *The New York Times* reports on its front page about spectacular experiments in the churches, and nationwide magazines like *Time* and *Newsweek* send reporters to progressive congregations for news coverage. It is one of the major goals of this volume to analyze this revolutionary change. It is something like a firsthand report of the process of change in American Protestantism.

And yet, this entire unrest in the churches would be sterile should it aim exclusively at the destruction or removal of the old forms. Fortunately, however, destruction or removal of the old is followed by the reconstruction of the parish in a new shape. The material to achieve this is of varying quality—the architects come from various schools

15

and there is no unanimously accepted style of architecture. However, all approaches to church renewal have one thing in common—they have been borne out of a joy and a supreme appreciation of experimentation. Thus the "ethos" of the reform work is articulated: experimentation as the life style of the church.

There is a significant parallel between the practical reform of the church and new approaches in theology in general. These two areas compete in radicalism with each other, raising decisive questions and trying appropriate solutions. Neither academic scholars nor practical reformers of the church are willing to regard traditional structures as everlasting or definite. The exchange of ideas and experiences occurs with freedom. This brings us to the second characteristic of the American church renewal: the inadequacy of traditional modes of thought and existing structures.

The third characteristic is marked by the passionate desire to turn the church inside out toward the world. The social-ethical dimension of American church renewal is obvious. It describes a theological farewell to the emphasis on individualism in the American Protestantism of the past. The concept of the German theologian Dietrich Bonhoeffer that the Christian existence ought to be an existence "for others" has been adopted by American church reformers in an impressive way. Bonhoeffer's ideas yield concrete results in contemporary church renewal. Hence, the third distinguishing mark of the reform work can be formulated: contemporary church renewal gets its driving power from the conviction that the church ought to display ethical responsibility for society.

SURVEY OF THE REFORM MOVEMENT

All phenomena of the reform movement put together can be compared with the organism of an orchestra. The polyphony and rich instrumentation are directed from a central point, i.e. from the conductor, yielding a harmonious wholeness. It might be said that the various concepts of church renewal are all conducted by the same fruitful restlessness in the search for a new structure. The attempt is to integrate single contributions into a whole picture. This has developed on at least six levels.

1. THE RENEWAL OF THE PARISH STRUCTURE. When exposed to this approach, forms of Christian fellowship in a certain geographical area (parish) undergo drastic changes. The first part of this book will deal with this subject in detail.

2. SPECIALIZED MINISTRIES. Parallel with the restructuring of the parish, specialized services of the church in different areas of contemporary society have gained in importance. Specially trained ministers have left the residential parish behind and have turned to the shopping center, to the deserted streets of American cities by night, to the realm of government, or to the coffeehouse. The second part of the present volume describes this shift in pastoral emphasis.

3. CENTERS OF SPIRITUAL RENEWAL. Included in this category are all Christian communities of fellowship whose origins lie in the monastic life of the early church. With certain modifications, we encounter these days the reappearance of that primitive fellowship structure in the so-called retreat centers. These academy-like institutions are located in unpopulated areas to guarantee the highest possible concentration and alertness for Bible studies. The purpose of these centers of spiritual renewal is the devotional edification of the participants. Around these centers there have been established noticeable fellowship groups, nonparochial in character. The practical pietism of these groups is a considerable contribution to the renewal of the highly structured traditional church, since they regain the charismatic element lost in the process of institutionalization. Two American examples of these centers of Christian renewal [1] which

[1] Donald Bloesch, *Centers of Christian Renewal* (Philadelphia: United Church Press, 1964). See also Colin W. Williams, "A New Monasticism?" *Where in the World?* (New York: National Council of Churches, 1963), p. 109. Francois Biot, O.P., *The Rise of Protestant Monasticism* (Baltimore: Helicon Press, 1963).

have parallels in the *Iona Community* in Scotland and the *Taizé Brotherhood* in France are the *Yokefellow Institute* in Richmond, Indiana, and *Kirkridge* in Bangor, Pennsylvania.

4. TRAINING INSTITUTES. In recent years the church has become more concerned with the need to participate in the revolution of the entire educational system. Hence, the church has recognized that education or—on a more practical level—training will determine her shape in the last third of this century. As a matter of fact, a great number of institutions for continuing religious education have been set up in the last decade for both officers of the church and laymen. In making these efforts American churches have adopted the structure of the Evangelical Academy, which came into existence in postwar Germany. Moreover, American training institutes have surpassed the German original in developing curricula that bring about the trainee's involvement in the learning process rather than feed him with lectures and discussion opportunities only, as it is the case in Germany.[2] At present America has the best training facilities throughout all the Oekumene for the church in the urban context. Three institutes particularly have gained national reputation.

The Ecumenical Institute in Chicago, founded by the Church Federation of Greater Chicago in 1957, provides the renewal movement with provocative concepts for the parochial structure in the society of the future. One of the characteristics of the institute is that its instructors are convinced that the church can be renewed only if the local congregation be retained as the starting point. The program of the Ecumenical Institute enriches the debate on new missionary structures more than people usually are willing to admit. The structure of the Institute itself is a cross section of a lay training institute and a research center. One of the

[2] Lee G. Gable, *Evangelical Academy and Parish in West Germany, 1945-1961* (Lancaster, Pa.: Lancaster Theological Seminary, 1962). Lee G. Gable, *Church and World Encounter* (Philadelphia: United Church Press, 1964).

staff members has put it in these words: "We are a laboratory for the church. You might compare us to the Research Center of the Ford Motor Company or Jewel Tea. We are searching for programs and testing projects that will update it for the twenty-first century."

The imaginative teaching methods of the Institute applied to weekend courses for lay people and special programs for clergymen in Chicago have been so successful that staff members not too long ago began to hold courses in other places all over the United States and even abroad—in Asia, Australia, and Europe.

The Urban Training Center in Chicago, which started to function in 1964, places a different emphasis on training. Here the city is the focus. The Urban Training Center wants to serve as a supplement to seminary training that proved inadequate in the preparation of young men for the ministry in an urban setting. During a very demanding and sometimes robust curriculum the trainee is exposed to all possible urban situations that later might become problems in his ministry. He learns to get acquainted with the urban power structure; he is instructed how to recognize priorities in his ministry, and how to expand his skills for the best of his parish and the city. Through it all the trainee gathers valuable experiences for his church back home.

Metropolitan Urban Service Training (MUST) [3] in New York, unlike its counterpart in Chicago, is more concerned with mastering the metropolitan challenge to the church theologically. It began its first program in late 1966 under the leadership of George W. Webber who had been working until then in the East Harlem Protestant Parish. In an early position paper the MUST staff specified its goal in comparison to the Urban Training Center in Chicago: "Whereas the Urban Training Center in Chicago was designed to bring the clergy from all over the country for retraining in urban ministry and for the development of

[3] MUST was initiated by the Board of Missions of The United Methodist Church.

specialized skills for city church work, MUST has a mandate to challenge the resources of Christian faith and obedience for a more effective service in the metropolitan area. . . . It is the function of MUST to highlight urban problems where the Christian is needed, and to provide the training which will enable him to meet the challenge effectively."

Hence, the curriculum includes courses in which the student learns how to organize and operate a Job Opportunity Center. He also gets involved in community action programs and fund-raising techniques, and he learns how to use individual and collective power. A Student Intern Program widens the range of interest and involvement in the metropolitan focus of MUST. Meanwhile the National Division of The United Methodist Board of Missions has submitted another plan, called MUST II, which, in contrast to MUST I, will develop a training program for both the rural *and* the urban setting.

5. CHURCH PLANNING. This aspect of the broad renewal movement in American Protestantism takes professionally into consideration the increase in regional planning. Regionalism is "an aggregate of functional economic areas with a common orientation." [4] Accordingly, church planning studies the impact of geographical, economic, and social factors upon the formation of community life in a certain area. Church planning, in other words, investigates what the most adequate locations for the foundation for new churches are. Church planning also entails ecumenical cooperation between the denominations.[5] Walter Kloetzli has made an excellent survey of the history of research and planning in a basic paper[6] in which he also quotes the aims of church

[4] *Ecumenical Design. Imperatives for Action in Non-Metropolitan America* (New York: The National Consultation on the Church in Community Life, 1967), p. 180.

[5] The best survey at present in this field has been made by Lyle E. Schaller, *Planning for Protestantism in Urban America* (Nashville: Abingdon Press, 1965).

[6] Perry L. Norton, ed., *Search: A Report of the National Consultation of Personnel Needs in Church Planning and Research* (New York: National Council of Churches, 1960), pp. 20-41.

planning as defined in 1941 by the Federal and Home Mission Councils: "the formulation of a comprehensive strategy of church extension and maintenance for regions and communities, applying equally to the self-supporting and to mission-aided churches, for the primary purpose of insuring a well-rounded Christian ministry, according to our highest standards and ideals, to the entire population." [7] Today many church federations and councils of churches have a staff of professional planners who work and make decisions in close cooperation with theologians and ministers.

6. ORGANIZING METROPOLITAN MISSION. The dominating social context for contemporary American church work is the city. By now about 75 percent of the total population of the United States is living in about 200 metropolitan areas; this figure was 69.9 percent in 1960. In 1900 not more than 39.7 percent of the American people lived in the cities. With the focus on the urban setting the church follows the ranking of priorities in political and cultural affairs. During recent years it has become apparent that the church in her existence is utterly dependent upon the rise and the fall of the American city. Progressive theologians and laymen discerned that the only effective way to come to grips with the major problems of this development would be a completely new approach to urban church work. Four major types of metropolitan cooperation have emerged.

1) Metropolitan Councils and Church Federations. They rest heavily on the support of the local congregation. The latter sends its representatives to the council so that the local congregations are the constituent bodies. They represent only the parish, not the denomination. According to Moore and Day "there are generally two categories of programs: activities that serve the local churches, and those that provide direct services to people." [8]

[7] Ibid., p. 35.
[8] Urban Church Breakthrough (New York: Harper, 1966), p. 123. See also a description of how the Cleveland Council of Churches operates, pp. 128-31.

2) Metropolitan Indicatories. Denominational missions or judicatories are designed to serve the metropolitan area for a single denomination only. On this point they differ from the interdenominational councils. They do not, however, differ as far as the goal is concerned—the urban setting is still the major context for operation. Or, as Grace Ann Goodman puts it: "Most denominations have some unit that covers all or part of a metropolitan area, such as a Presbytery, a City Missionary Society, a Diocese. It is this unit that finds itself dealing with questions of racial justice, poverty, housing, on behalf of all its congregations . . . and it is this unit that has the mandate to administer, research, and plan strategy for the 'conventional' ministries of church nurture, education, and mission in this area." [9]

3) New Forms of Ecumenical Cooperation. Independent from the forms of cooperation mentioned above, new patterns of joint missionary action have developed since 1964. They are outnumbered by the interdenominational councils in terms of participating denominations or churches, yet they surpass these councils in efficiency and determination to perform contemporary strategy for mission. "Getting a job done is the primary goal; if unity is manifested, that's an additional attraction. A result of this assumption that the new ecumenical groups do not set out to attract and include all possible denominations; they gather those who are ready to act and do not worry about being totally representative." [10] As Grace Goodman shows in the paper mentioned, six examples of this new operation style can be found in New York City, Rochester, Syracuse, Los Angeles, Cleveland, and Chicago.

4) Joint Action in Mission on the National Level. The most promising effort made so far by any single denomination is the *Joint Urban Program* of the Executive Council of the Episcopal Church. Started in 1964, this project has

[9] *New Forms for Ecumenical Cooperation for Mission in Metropolitan Areas* (New York: Institute of Strategic Studies, Board of National Missions, United Presbyterian Church, USA, 1967), p. 1.
[10] *Ibid.*

22

resulted in the development of a forceful bond of communication between the denomination and its constituency. One of the media in this communication bond is the magazine *Church in Metropolis,* which has shown that from both the theological and the journalistic standpoint this project is really in touch with the major items crucial for the establishment of a concerted metropolitan mission.[11] The Joint Urban Program is designed to work out patterns of metropolitan mission in all major cities. The presiding bishop, John E. Hines, wrote of this project: "The Joint Urban Program of the Executive Council, during the past triennium, may be seen as the beginning of a major national effort on the part of this church to develop more effective forms and patterns of mission and ministry."[12] An even stronger emphasis was made on this program when in 1967 the United Church of Christ and the United Presbyterian Church joined the Episcopal Church for what is called *Joint Action in Urban Mission.* This committee submitted proposals for joint planning in mission on the national and regional level.

THE CHARACTER OF THIS STUDY

This study concentrates on the first two areas of church renewal mentioned earlier—i.e., the reconstruction of the congregation, and forms of specialized ministries. Yet it does not claim to provide a general survey of church life in America. Instead the purpose is to analyze experiments performed during the past ten years. Hence, no description is given of the traditionally structured congregation or parish. Only those phenomena have been considered that may be called avant-garde in structure and function. Briefly, the study is concerned with the "church in experiment."

Within this framework the account will pursue a two-

[11] See the special volume of *Church in Metropolis,* Fall, 1967, which gives a survey of the first three years of the Joint Urban Program.

[12] *Ibid.,* p. 3.

fold purpose. On one side it analyzes the avant-garde church. In order to do this, I got in touch with some of these churches personally; others I knew from persons participating in experimental church work. Surprisingly, during the collection of material it became apparent that America, where bold experimentation is going to become the life style of the church, has not yet produced a comprehensive study or a conceptual framework for the discussion on church renewal.[13] Thus, this present book attempts to fill a gap caused by the absence of descriptive and analytical studies in this field. It addresses the layman and theologian alike. I also want to encourage more discussions in congregations and seminaries. It is, among other publications, a first step to what I am convinced will arise sooner or later—a systematic study of church renewal.[14]

Understandably, one of the major tasks has been to collect case studies, which are spread over dozens of journals, magazines, newspapers, pamphlets, and books. In addition I have exchanged many letters with clergymen working with experiments. The denominational headquarters proved to be an especially helpful source for gathering empirical studies of single experiments. The material stemming from both of these sources finally has been put together in order to design a general picture. This brings me to the second major purpose of this book.

It has been necessary to categorize the manifold experi-

[13] I know only two books relatively comprehensive in character, yet not enough. One is Richard E. Moore and Duane L. Day, *Urban Church Breakthrough;* the other is M. Edward Clark, William L. Malcomson, Warren Lane Molton, *The Church Creative: A Reader on the Renewal of the Church* (Nashville: Abingdon Press, 1967). In England a study on the same subject appeared recently.

[14] A major administrative step toward a systematic study of church renewal was made in the summer of 1967 when the Division of Christian Life and Mission of the National Council of Churches got a Director for Experimental Ministries, who at present is Frank P. White, a graduate of Yale Divinity School. In 1968, Mr. White was evaluating a nationwide questionnaire of persons involved in experimental ministries. Mr. White has also compiled information on church renewal and has built up a remarkable file about the fruitful unrest in the churches.

ments. In view of the fact that no similar task had been undertaken, that has proved difficult. Hence, the conceptualization is yet incomplete. Here and there improvement will be made by subsequent studies. Yet, for the time being the author wants to spare any observer of church renewal that kind of frustration so many people experience—confusion, the absence of clarity, and even discouragement in looking at so many different starting points. The conceptual framework of this volume, therefore is meant to be something like a machine with which one can make his way through the jungle of church renewal.

Because of a restriction in space and material the reader may be disappointed not to find all examples described in detail. I am aware of this lack; I hope nevertheless, I can pass this inefficiency to the reader himself for further improvement, encouraging him to do more research in the direction he wants to go.

This lack of completeness, however, has advantages. The greater the condensation of material, the more quickly the reader can become informed. Again, the strength of this study is not the exhaustive description of models and experiments in church renewal; rather it is the analysis of the broad range of church renewal with the sketching of examples as illustrations. Thus, the reader will get the most out of this book by studying the presented material within a short period.

THE LACK OF A CONCEPTUAL FRAMEWORK

Before us a new shape of the church in the second half of the twentieth century is emerging. And yet, how many laymen and theologians are intensively aware of this revolutionary process? The first period of wild experimentation is over. It is time now to deal with the destruction and reconstruction of church forms on an academic level, too. What is needed most is a scientific examination of all these phenomena. In this respect a real pioneering work has yet to be achieved. It is hard to comprehend how the theological offspring of universities and seminaries can be concerned with church renewal in a more systematic way, unless a conceptual framework plus an adequate phraseology is at hand. The task before practical theology is the development of what might be called a "sociology of mission." It would deal with the sociological exploration of the new concepts of mission presented in recent years by the World Council of Churches and its American working group. "Sociology of mission" would be designed in close relationship to "theology of mission." However, the "sociology of mission" would not expand the work done in the field of the sociology of the parish. Rather, it would proceed toward a sociology of the missionary proclamation in general. The leading question of a sociology of mission would be: What are the structural and social implications of the missionary activity performed by new congregations and experimenting ministries? In the search for an appropriate answer to this question lies the pioneering task of any practical theology in the future.

PART I
STRUCTURES AND FUNCTIONS OF THE CONGREGATION

1
Factors of Parish Versatility

What is parish versatility? Using this term here we understand it to be the way the congregation relates its activities to a specific location serving as the geographical starting point for mission. In other words, the question is raised as to how the building facilities of the parish need to be arranged if the congregation wants to be versatile for mission! Hence, the degree to which parish versatility is developed is dependent upon the selection of the location for parish activities. Of course, a congregation can be very successful operating with the traditionally designed church building that has always been located on a fixed place bound to a certain location. Yet, in general, it is the rule that the efficacy of the missionary function of the congregation will vary with the decentralization and secularization of those places where the congregation meets and worships.

The presupposition for all these considerations—and for the practical experiments later described in detail as well —is a revolutionary new concept of mission according to which the church *is* mission, rather than mission understood only as the prolonged arm of congregational activity. Mission is no longer merely the most emphasized of the usual church activities, it is the core of congregational life.[1]

---

[1] The "chief ideologist" of the new concept of mission is the Dutch theologian and former missionary J. C. Hoekendijk. In his book *The Church Inside Out* (Philadelphia: Westminster Press, 1964), which

29

In the background of this new approach to mission, parish versatility becomes one of the crucial issues. If mission does not serve any longer as one function in competition with several others, but rather becomes *the* function of the congregation, then the selection of church locations and the circumstances for gathering reveal simply the self-understanding of the congregation. Hence, the strategic starting point of mission and the geographical center for the total life of the congregation are inextricably related to one another. Hoekendijk writes:

In church building a shift ought to take place from *sacral architecture* to the designing of a *fellowship house*. . . . A shift *from cathedral to chapel* must take place in our church building. The cathedral is symbolic of a stable society. . . . The chapel is the movable house. . . . In our church building a shift ought to take place *from "the church at the center" to an addition to the new housing development of our society.* In our buildings too it must become clear that the church has "no permanent city" here.[2]

We discover in the reform movement for church renewal something like an "exodus tradition." According to this tradition, scholars say, we find in the first books of the Bible themes that refer to the escape of the ancient Israelites from Egypt. This event was afterwards celebrated enthusiastically in their rites each year. One of the literal expressions of this event of salvation is the so-called exodus theme, helping subsequent generations to remember what happened in the beginning of their history. Finally it became the "exodus tradition," the tradition of telling the old narratives.

Today this exodus theme is actualized in an altered way in the new concepts of mission. The church is called to cooperation with society to participate in the great social, cultural, and political tasks before us. For this purpose the

---

is a collection of articles over the last 15 years, he sets the criteria for the future missionary task of the local congregation in a prophetic language. Cf. esp. pp. 32-46.

[2] *Ibid.,* pp. 82-84.

church is asked to emigrate from her self-constructed cave in order to escape her contemporary Egypt. Following this call the church strips off all shackles of the institution. This *theological* consideration is but one aspect. Another is the *sociological* structure of the exodus-mission task.

Versatility is a necessary characteristic for assimilation among social partners. We can distinguish several varieties of parish versatility, as the term is applied to missionary structures of the congregation.

THE UNILATERAL TYPE

The term "unilateral" is commonly used in sociology, especially in studies of kinship relations. It describes "descent and descent groups in which a single line of descent . . . is recognized as socially significant as a means of organizing such social activities and institutions as inheritance, ritual congregations." [3] It might appear inappropriate to use the term "unilateral" also in the area of church renewal. Yet, as mentioned above, the present development of the entire business of church renewal puts before us the task of creating a nomenclature appropriate to the various phenomena in the field of experimentation in the church. The objections of researchers in sociology notwithstanding, the attempt is made here to speak of the "unilateral versatility of the parish," conceptualizing that type of development of missionary functions which takes its point of departure from one central geographical place exclusively, like a residential church building. Within this "unilateral type" we again can distinguish two subtypes:

1. CHURCH-BUILDING-CENTERED. The traditionally structured parish retains its church building, though it remains flexible enough to direct from there a great variety of services to the community. *Judson Memorial Church* in New

[3] Julius Gould and William L. Kolb, *A Dictionary of the Social Sciences* (New York: The Free Press, 1964), p. 737.

York's Greenwich Village, the Latin Quarter of New York, is an example.[4] Right across from trim Judson's church building is Washington Square, a scene of action for hipsters, drug addicts, and the protest generation. To get in touch with these eccentric people of the community Judson Memorial turned against the deeply rooted ecclesiastical reservation toward artists and developed a completely new approach that years later turned out to be a model for contemporary church work among artists in America.[5] And yet the Reverend Howard Moody and his colleague have retained the church building for their style of progressive experimentation, since its geographical-strategic situation is simply ideal. One of Judson's members made this remark: "Judson is the sort of place which absorbs dramatic contradictions. There's something in the atmosphere here which makes it impossible for dichotomies to coexist—some sort of looseness. But it's also the Village. You couldn't have this church anywhere but in the Village." [6] Judson shows that parish versatility does not lead necessarily to the dismissal of the sacred building if its missionary-strategic location proves to be superior to every "profane" location.

2. PROFANE-BUILDING-CENTERED. A number of other congregations have abandoned the church building and have moved their sanctuary to secular locations.

The congregation of the *Methodist Inner City Parish in Kansas City*, believes that rented storefronts as starting points for church work serve the community better than

[4] Judson Memorial United Methodist Church is located at 55 Washington Square South, New York, N.Y. Specific data about the parish program are hard to get. Here are some reports that go more into detail than the present volume does. Howard Moody, "Toward a Religionless Church for a Secular World," *Who's Killing the Church?* Stephen C. Rose, ed. (New York: Association Press, 1966), pp. 82-92. *Union Seminary Quarterly Review*, March, 1966, pp. 328-33. *New York Times*, July 3, 1966. Sally Kempton, "Beatitudes at Judson Memorial Church," *Esquire*, March, 1966; *Newsweek*, April 7, 1969 (European edition), p. 46.

[5] For further details on the parish program cf. pp. 100-102.

[6] Kempton, "Beatitudes at Judson Memorial Church," p. 2.

hidden sanctuaries.[7] One of the storefronts of the parish is located at one of the major trouble spots in Kansas City. This area is the center of alcoholism, drug addiction, and prostitution. The neighborhood consists of housing units of substandard quality. On one side of the storefront is a tavern, on the other a cleaning establishment. A few years ago the people in this neighborhood lived in cold homes during the winter and went hungry. They lived in dwellings where the water, gas, and electricity had been shut off. Some died because of deprivation. Some were evicted and put out into the street. Babies lacked milk to keep their frail bodies alive. When they died there was no way of burying them decently. Against this background of despair and humiliation a social service program was developed by three struggling congregations, and carried on in the storefronts of the parish. Screened off at the rear of the room is the office where the secretarial work is performed for the entire parish. Also to the rear is a movable screen giving partial privacy to the social worker who interviews persons waiting in a long line. Several other desks out in the open serve as interview facilities. In the middle is a ping-pong table. Each night from 5:00 to 7:30 there is a recreation period. Between twelve and twenty children come to get involved in various recreational activities. Besides this there is opportunity in the storefront to get advice and help in all kinds of life situations.

The decision of this parish to choose storefronts entails a twofold consequence for parish versatility in general: (1) The church building is either replaced or supplemented by the profane building. (2) Parish versatility is still dependent upon a fixed and relatively permanent location.

THE MULTILATERAL TYPE

The third variation of parish versatility is characterized by a strict renunciation of any central and permanent lo-

[7] For further information see "Forging Alternatives to Slum Despair," *Together,* May, 1966, pp. 50-56.

cation for a congregation. "Multilateral" signifies flexibility
of location in relation to the developed parish versatility.
It operates from several different places. The biblical picture
of God's wandering people becomes a reality for those congregations.

Valley United Church of Christ in Concord, California,
came into existence when some persons decided in 1962 to
organize a church. The initial phase in the history of this
congregation was not different from many others. A parsonage was provided for the minister, and a lot was ac-
quired where later the church building would be constructed. But then something happened that was completely
against all rules of ordinary congregational development.
During these first years the congregation's concept of
church underwent a deep change. The vigor and intensity
of the discussion is well expressed in their statement:

The building requires us to keep our focus on *our* church,
our God, *ourselves.* Our buildings say the direct opposite of
what we believe. Our fellowship halls frequently are not open
to everyone. . . . As we look at the style of life which is
emerging in our society we note some radical changes. We
notice the great mobility in our suburban communities. When
the church builds its own structure under these changing circumstances, it is limiting flexibility.[8]

Since Valley United Church wanted to become a servant
church, it was decided not to build a church. The committed group of Christians in the California valley preferred
to do something for the good of their community rather
than being constantly concerned with the problems of fi-
nancing church buildings and running into troubles with
the provision of money for maintenance. Besides, the small
congregation could not afford a full-time minister, since
it counted on only 30 families in 1967. The Reverend William Smith made the decision that "I am seeking half-time
work in the world to help supplement what I need to
support my family. This is the type of model that the

[8] Report Form for New Forms of the Ministry, released by the
Board of Homeland Ministries, UCC.

clergyman will have to develop to carry on this type of ministry in the suburban community—it is too controversial and requires a higher level of personal involvement for the suburban mentality." [9]

The next step in the development of an appropriate structure was that the congregation proved what other (profane) buildings would fit the policy. At first the group gathered for worship in a high school. Later, Valley United Church designed a monthly schedule for a congregation that had decided *not* to be bound to a fixed ecclesiastical stronghold like a church building. The multilateral type of parish versatility is revealed in the variety of places for gathering: (1) The first Sunday evening of each month the congregation has its regular family worship service with dialogue-sermons. This takes place at a Baptist church. (2) On the second Sunday of each month the congregation concentrates on adult education. The group meets at the parsonage from eight until ten at night in programs that are designed to update the people theologically. (3) The third Sunday evening of each month is devoted to family Christian education. The congregation gathers as family units and shares in studies. (4) On the fourth Sunday evening Valley United Church gathers for a task force concern at the parsonage. At these meetings the question is raised where in the community the church ought to become involved and where it can promote social change and more humane conditions in the world.

This multilaterial type of parish versatility includes also the two factors analyzed in the preceeding section—that is, the church building and the profane building. It also supplements parish versatility through the multilateral element.

SUMMARY

We discerned three types of parish versatility:

1. Versatility that takes as its starting point a geographically fixed church building.

[9] From a letter to the author.

2. Versatility that rests heavily upon a profane building instead of a church building. However, a fixed and relatively permanent location, non-sacred in character, is retained (unilateral).

3. Versatility that is determined by the decentralization of meeting places. Several different places, non-sacred in character and varied in architecture, provide the setting for the missionary activity of the congregation (multilateral).

2
Locations for Gathering

THE HIGH-RISE CHURCH

What is a high-rise church? Certainly it is not a church dozens of stories high, a revival of the medieval cathedral that was built exclusively to praise the Lord in stone and plaster. Rather it is a sober design, far more functional than the architects of Chartres, Cologne, and Coventry intended. Whereas for Gothic architecture the glory of God has been the motive for building churches, for the construction of twentieth-century "high-rise churches" utility and calculative considerations are the ultimate concerns. Thus, we may try now to give a definition of what is called the high-rise church. The high-rise church is the transformation of the traditional church building into a combination of apartment or office building with a sanctuary. The architecture of this high-rise church is no longer determined exclusively by the purpose of providing an architectural framework for liturgical functions, but rather has been exposed to the functionalism of modern life, in this case to the residential and vocational area.

Trinity Temple United Methodist Church in Louisville, Kentucky[1] had to make a major decision in 1957. The old church building of that congregation, wedged in among the commercial towers of Louisville's inner city, was in bad shape. It needed $100,000 in repairs, and that kind of money could not be afforded. But someone had a splendid idea. Why

[1] See *Together,* February, 1964, p. 54.

not provide income property to help pay the cost of building a new church? In other words, the means to the end of constructing a new church building was the invention of an experimental form, the high-rise church. The church borrowed $2,575,000 on a 40-year loan basis and built a 196-foot building, topped by a 20-foot cross, at the place where the old church had been torn down. At the street level are the sanctuary and meeting rooms and on the roof a glass-walled chapel. The 14 floors between have 72 one-bedroom apartments and 146 efficiencies that rent from $94 to $132 a month (in 1964). For the first time a church sanctuary and a chapel were architecturally integrated in the style of modern housing.

Trinity Towers—the name of the new construction—is an excellent point of departure for almost every type of missionary response to all kinds of needs: apartment-house ministry, community service programs (Trinity Towers has a central location in the inner city), ministry to the commercial sector, and so forth. In this connection it might be interesting to mention that Louisville's Trininty Towers has a predecessor in Chicago. There the over 50-year-old Chicago Temple housing the First United Methodist Church is a provocative contrast to the modern administration buildings in the inner city. This building—in the upper part a neo-gothic steeple, in the lower part an office facade —has also a sanctuary on street level and another worship place on top of the building. Today this church building-office-skyscraper combination still is among the highest buildings of downtown Chicago.

While the type described as high-rise church still shows the marks of the traditional sacred structure, the model to be analyzed next can be regarded as a radical breaking with the tradition of church building construction.

HOMES AND PUBLIC BUILDINGS

There are indications that a revival of the ancient house-church idea lies before us. Generally speaking, in the entire business of church renewal all "mini" structures seem to be of utmost attractiveness, instead of the outmoded "macro" structures of the institution. The most neglected, yet oldest type of those mini-structures, is the house church or the church in the house. J. C. Hoekendijk, the Dutch theologian and enfant terrible in the field of mission, writes: "Since about 1950, attention has been given to this phenomenon in various countries of Europe, but we do not really want to face it."[2] The second part of this sentence is apparently a cynical remark against those who, although foreseeing that the expansion of the house church would challenge the "sanctuary church" unprecedentedly, notoriously deny the revolutionary power of the house church renaissance. We, on our part, do better to be reminded of the fact that one of the revolutions in post-Reformation church history, the emergence of Pietism in Germany and England, yielded as one of its by-products the revival of the house church, which in some places turned the overtly structured church establishment upside down.

It was also in Europe, especially in England, that—no longer than twenty-five years ago—the modern house-church movement came into existence. Edwin H. Robertson has given a brief and excellent survey of the revival of the house-church idea.[3] Toward the end of his article Robertson writes: "The house churches are a protest; but this protest may be a beginning of the renewal of the church." [4] Probably the most outspoken advocate of the house church today is Hans-Ruedi Weber, a former missionary to Indonesia and later active in the World Council of Churches. He says:

Perhaps the most important is the rediscovery of the New Testament house church. The early Christian Church lived

[2] *The Church Inside Out*, p. 91.
[3] *The House Church, Basileia. Walter Freytag zum 60. Geburtstag.* Jan Hermelink and H. J. Margull, eds. (Stuttgart: Evangelisches Verlagswerk, 1959).
[4] *Ibid.*, p. 371.

and grew essentially in and through house congregations. Whereas the oikos, the concrete social milieu, mostly consisted at that time of the patriarchal family of antiquity, today the "house" can be the neighborhood in the place dimension or group in the work dimension (university church, factory church, etc.). What is essential is that the house church should be a small group within an existing or still-to-be-created observable community of life or work.[5]

How does the vanguard in the American renewal movement today interpret the meaning of the old word oikos? Here are some answers. Two major types have developed:

1. GATHERING OF CONGREGATIONS IN HOMES. Although there are many house churches existing in Protestant homes all over the country, the following illustration is taken from the Roman Catholic Church in order to demonstrate the gap between the church as an institution and the church as an experiencing and venturing fellowship group.

According to *The New York Times*[6] a group of twenty-four Roman Catholics gathered on Sunday, September 17, 1967, in *an apartment in Highland Park, New Jersey.* Instead of attending a conventional mass they preferred to convene in the way the early Christians did. The Reverend George J. Hafner moved forward on the sofa and carefully emptied a bottle of white wine into sixteen glasses on the coffee table before him. A student assisted him in distributing the glasses to the circle of worshipers, while others passed a wooden tray containing slices of whole-wheat bread. As they ate the bread and drank the wine they began to sing to the beat of a guitar:

> Sons of God, hear this holy Word!
> Gather 'round the Table of the Lord!
> Eat his body drink his Blood,
> And we will sing a song of Love:
> Allelu, allelu, allelu, alleluia!

[5] "The Marks of an Evangelizing Church," *The Missionary Church in East and West,* ed. Charles West *et al.* (London: S.C.M. Press, 1959), p. 113.

[6] Edward B. Fiske, "Suspended Priest Continues Banned Rites," *The New York Times,* September 18, 1967.

The group, most of them in their late twenties or early thirties, then formed a circle. Father Hafner, who was wearing a simple black suit and clerical collar, began by explaining the purpose of the service to newcomers; "We seek an alternative to the large impersonal parish and the kind of intimate Eucharistic observance described in the Gospels," he said. "We also want to show that there are varieties of ways to express the central truths of the liturgy."

For an hour the house congregation discussed why they were there. For almost all, the reason was lack of meaning in the normal liturgy. Worship then continued with a short variation of the sacrament of penance. Father Hafner then asked the congregation to pray silently and to declare their sorrow to God for their sins. He finally pronounced absolution and dismissed the congregation.

This house-church "happening" took place in the apartment of a twenty-seven-year-old chemist and was in almost every respect contrary to what the official church regarded as church renewal. The reaction on the bishop's side came promptly. A week before the house-church meeting described here—the group used to do that many times before —the Most Reverend George W. Ahr, bishop of Trenton, suspended Father Hafner for resigning his post as a parish priest in order to lead the new congregation. In the light of this earlier ban, Father Hafner's performance in the Highland Park apartment was open rebellion against the high church structure in which he had been raised.

How can house churches that are sprawled over a certain area avoid losing contact with one another? This is a crucial question put before all advocates of church gatherings in private homes. A solution to that problem can make this experimental structure (a 2,000-year-old one!) one of the most attractive forms of modern church life. An interesting proposal was submitted by Valley United Church of Christ mentioned earlier.[7] In a position paper the Christians in that California valley made the proposal to develop the house-church concept in the total Concord area. They pro-

[7] See p. 34.

41

posed to ask the Denominational Extension Department (UCC) to provide leadership aid for new house churches to be placed in Ygnacio Valley and in the West Concord area. The ministers and the lay people of the parish churches would see the Concord area and the central county as their parish. They would carry on a united program of service to the community while nurturing the local house-church members in depth. The house churches would gather together for corporate worship in a central spot, which they would rent. The individual groups would meet in their homes for nurture and depth experience. The members from all house churches together would share in their task force ministry to the community (in the areas of poverty, race relations, and so forth). These forms could be developed alongside the traditional parish program.

Two major elements of contemporary church renewal are amalgamated in this proposal, an older and a more recent one. The older one was articulated in a classical way by George W. Webber:

. . . the center of the life of the church must not simply be the worship on Sunday morning. . . . We must participate in the common worship life of the congregation and we must also participate in a group within that life of the whole congregation. . . . We join in congregational worship. We meet in small groups. . . . This new focus in the life of the colony [i.e., the church in the diaspora] goes under many different names: cell group, study group, house meetings, and so on.[8]

The more recent element is the idea of the "church in the region." This concept stemmed from the studies in the World Council of Churches and became popular especially in Europe. The Western European Working Group,[9] for example, speaks of *zonal structures* and substantiates the use of that word saying that "the term is

[8] *God's Colony in Man's World* (Nashville: Abingdon Press, 1960), pp. 58-59.
[9] *Planning for Mission, Working Papers on the New Quest for Missionary Communities,* ed. by Thomas Wieser (New York: The U.S. Conference for the W.C.C., 1966).

used to describe a territorial area within which by and large the population lives out the complex network of movement and relationship which is its life. A zone thus comprehends and integrates most of the various contexts around which the population is concentrated for the basic activities of local life." [10] The Working Group furthermore speaks of the "emergence of regional thinking," which means that people living in a zone become conscious of the functions of interdependent factors. The implications for the church are considerable. It is asked to develop forms of interdenominational cooperation and to make use of larger units for major policy decisions and for administrations.

Gathering in homes is but one aspect of the house-church boom. Other congregations have interpreted the house-church emphasis in a different way. They come together in public buildings instead of private homes.

2. GATHERING OF CONGREGATIONS IN PUBLIC BUILDINGS. On a November night in the fall of 1965 a deep crisis began to shake the *First Congregational Church in Elmhurst, Illinois.* According to an article appearing a short time later, this church once was the prestige church in Elmhurst. After the majority of church members, which consisted of conservatives, complained that the incumbent minister had not given enough attention to card clubs, ladies clubs, and the normal church business, and decided to fire him, a split in the congregation occurred. Those who felt that they should stay in this congregation formed a new church, which they called "The Church of the New Covenant." And this was the agenda for the remnant:

We want no building, now or in the future. We shall rent space as we now rent the chapel of Elmhurst College. The building we left had proved to be the master of the old congregation. If it is humanly possible, church buildings are to be dispensed with. If the fellowship breaks down, there should be as little brick and mortar as possible to hold the group together when the spirit has fled. We realize this cannot be

[10] *Ibid.,* p. 210.

43

a universal course, but since it appears that we can do without property, we are overjoyed at the prospect. Freed of this burden, we have decided that, at a bare minimum, one half of the church budget must go to missions outside the church.[11]

As this Elmhurst remnant, emerging from the split with the old "brick-building" congregation, convenes on a college campus, the congregation described next gathers in a restaurant. In 1962 an Episcopal minister started in the southwest of Washington, D.C., an apartment-house ministry that was gradually transformed into a congregation with its own church building. *St. Augustine Episcopal Chapel* tried several new structures before it became a residential congregation. One of the first experiments in the series was that the congregation gathered in a restaurant, since the apartments proved to be not large enough to provide a worship place. In this restaurant nonconformist approaches to make liturgy more meaningful were realized. Ignoring the standard Episcopal practice, the minister introduced this small congregation to the idea that every worship service contains both preaching the word and celebrating the sacrament. "Communion is the celebration of the life of Christ in the world," he commented. "We have lost the feeling of celebration, the ecstatic part in life. We tend to start reforms by trying to make the service more imaginative, when we should be working from the other end, working the liturgy in the world. It is a function of the church to point out to people and identify and celebrate the worship going on in life in the world. A most obvious way today is in the Freedom movement. I went to Montgomery, Alabama, on the voting right march—that was a whole day of worship." [12]

Starting with this basic understanding of liturgy in the contemporary world, the group made three innovations:

[11] Ron Goetz, "The Power of Negative Action," *Renewal* magazine, March, 1966, p. 7.

[12] Grace Ann Goodman, *The Church and the Apartmenthouse* (New York: Board of National Missions, United Presbyterian Church USA, 1966), p. 63.

(1) As the group was meeting in a restaurant they could arrange the chairs there any way they liked. Hence, they shifted to a three-sided seating arrangement with the table in the middle. (2) In the regular Prayer for the Whole State of Christ's Church the minister used two pauses at certain sections to encourage members of the congregation to share with the whole group spontaneously matters of personal or community concerns. The congregation also used ordinary bread and wine (which is not consecrated). (3) To illustrate his sermons and prayers, the minister made use of audio-visual devices, such as slides. Every six weeks an "instructed service" was held at which a layman, previously assigned to prepare comments on the meaning of various elements of the liturgy, was asked to stop the service to give his explanations at whatever points he chose.

St. Augustine's Episcopal Chapel is one of those interesting ventures in church renewal which tried several ways of experimentation before it found its identity, its future shape as a residential congregation.

Apart from the high-rise church and private and public buildings, there are also locations in commercial buildings that serve as places for congregational gathering. A widespread representative for this type is the storefront church in all its variations.

COMMERCIAL BUILDINGS

The storefront church is the ideal device for the communication of mission in our time. If the church gets out of the "store *rear*," so to speak, to the "store *front*" it lets people know that the period of the "public" existence of the church has dawned and that at the same time the era of private faith has come to an end. In a storefront the church exhibits its nature to the world. So far the use of the storefront by the church has taken on three forms: (1) the storefront converted, (2) the Christian coffeehouse, (3) the shopping-center church.

First of all, most storefronts serve as locations from which congregations carry out *social work*. This was the case, for example, in the Methodist Inner City Parish in Kansas City.[13] Some other congregations also use the storefront to house their *church office*. The East Harlem Protestant Parish has its church office in a storefront located in a thickly populated area of New York at Second Avenue. And finally, there are storefronts used as centers for the whole parish life or even as places to hold *worship services*.

1. THE STOREFRONT CONVERTED. As everywhere, people in Winston-Salem, North Carolina, felt no longer challenged by the established church; rather they were bored by its irrelevance in liturgy and proclamation. And yet, the people there differed from the rest of upset churchgoers in the country who only complain and do not act. The unrest in Winston-Salem was organized toward a fruitful protest against the establishment in the church and transformed into a structure. It was a structured protest. The *Experimental Church of Winston-Salem*[14] which came into existence as a result, is located downtown in a Negro neighborhood and an urban renewal area. It has no chimes, no steeple, no organ, no preaching service, no Sunday school but it has a storefront.

In this building there is room enough for lectures, for the printing shop of the small newspaper, for teaching girls from the neighborhood domestic skills. This experimental church is a five-year project sponsored by the Winston-Salem Presbytery. The congregation is composed of Quakers, Baptists, Methodists, and Presbyterians. They all try to organize the people of the area where the storefront is located into an effective community. This congregation does not plan to build a permanent church building. It wants instead to serve wherever need requires immediate action.

[13] See pp. 32-33.
[14] Stephen M. Burns, "Church Without a Roof," *Christian Herald*, July, 1967, p. 19.

The pastor in charge of this North Carolina adventure, the Reverend James O. Chatham, Jr., had only critical remarks for the church establishment:

Traditional religion has assumed that to upbuild the church is to witness to God. This is the biggest fallacy in religion, I have ever heard. Almost every conventional church in this country has concerned itself with buying a piece of property in a fashionable neighborhood, building a beautiful sanctuary and filling its membership rolls with tithing members. It tells itself that as soon as these necessities . . . are taken care of, it will begin ministering to the needs of the community. The only problem is, these needs are never met.[15]

How does the Experimental Church meet these needs? First of all, by teaching its twenty members (in the summer of 1967). This teaching emphasis is prior to worship or meditation. Since the major concern in this small group lies in the involvement of the Christian in secular affairs, it is important to answer the questions, *Why* are they doing so, and *what* can they do in the future? Another "squadron" of this underground church is already active in the investigation of housing requirements for those who must be relocated from substandard housing to standard housing but do not have sufficient financial resources.

Most people probably would ask: how can these twenty Christians still claim to be the disciples of the Lord if they do not even have a worship service? And yet, although this is a very legitimate question, the Experimental Church is probably closer to the Pauline letter to the Romans than many churches with costly and nice-looking buildings. "I beg you, therefore, brothers, in view of God's mercies, that you present your bodies a living sacrifice, holy and acceptable to God—your worship with understanding." [16]

Let us finally recapitulate what this church has to offer and what it does not have. It *has*: social missionary service, community teaching, and membership instruction. It has *not*: a worship service, Sunday school, and club life.

[15] *Ibid.*, p. 65.
[16] Romans 12:1-2, from the Berkeley Version in Modern English.

Storefronts are not exclusively "reaction bureaus." They also serve as places for worship. What happens when a conventional congregation chooses an unconventional place for worship?

A business building in *Milwaukee's* Juneau Village houses the *Village Church,* sponsored partly by the Lutheran Church of America. In a meeting place with $11,000 per year rent and 2,650 square feet of space, the pastor, Dr. Eric J. Gustavson, serves a church that has no steeple, but apartments on top of its "roof." The church meeting in this expensive storefront hopes to develop a reputation for a center of spiritual renewal for apartment-house dwellers and the adjacent stores. "Well, you have a bank, an insurance firm, a restaurant and bar, a pharmacy . . . why not a church?" is the counterquestion pastor Gustavson snaps back to people surprised about finding the church on the main street of the twentieth century.[17]

Although Village Church came into existence to function as the "first church in the Lutheran Church in America that has been specifically organized to serve a high rise apartment community," [18] for our purpose here it can illustrate well enough how churches conduct their functions in a converted storefront. For Village Church the storefront is converted into a worship place. Converted here means not that the architecture as such has been changed but that the assumption of the contractor has been transformed. Instead of a businessman making a profit, a minister moves in to proclaim there the grace of God that comes gratis.

The congregation, established in 1966, has a minimum of structural organization. It has a council, a local committee for stewardship and worship, a "community committee" concerned with the political and social life of the city, and a "world committee" concerned with global questions. For the people of the surrounding apartment house buildings, a visit to the church has become like a walk to the pharmacy

[17] *The Lutheran* magazine, January 31, 1968, pp. 5-8.
[18] *Ibid.,* p. 6.

or to the restaurant. One of the fifty-six charter members of Village Church responded to this non-sacred location thus: "The worship and the discussion groups here present religion as it ought to be geared to modern living." And the head of Juneau Village Management said of the congregation: "They are doing a fine job."

2. THE CHRISTIAN COFFEEHOUSE. As the converted storefront serves manifold purposes of the congregation, the next storefront combination, the "Christian coffeehouse," fulfills one primary function—it supplies a place for dialogue between the church and the young generation, artists, and intellectuals in general. It is not the place here to discuss the specific characteristics of the Christian coffeehouse in detail; this will be done in Part Two.[19] At this place only one function of the Christian coffeehouse—to serve as a worship place—can be discussed. But why deal with the same subject at two separate places? The reason is that the Christian coffeehouse is a meeting and worship place for the *congregation,* as well as a structure of what may be called *functional mission*[20]—a service of the church in a certain area ministering in a special style of mission to people with specific interests and specific vocations.

How did the splendid idea, to serve God in a coffeehouse, come into existence, and how was it realized? Elizabeth O'Connor describes in her book on the Church of the Saviour in Washington, D.C.,[21] how it happened:

In the winter of 1958 Gordon [Gordon Cosby is the minister of the church] was invited to be the guest Lenten speaker at a church in New England. Mary [his wife] described the church as "dismal" and the congregation as "shivering." . . . When the service was over that night he and Mary drove a long way. They finally stopped at a small hotel where the last vacant room was above a tavern. Noisy voices and gay jukebox melodies drifted into their room and kept them from sleeping. Re-

19 See pp. 171-75.
20 See p. 131.
21 *Call to Commitment* (New York: Harper, 1963).

flecting on the sounds below and the church they left behind, Gordon recollected: "I realized that there was no more warmth and fellowship in that tavern than there was in the church. If Jesus of Nazareth had His choice, He would probably have come to the tavern rather than to the church we visited."

The next morning they had breakfast at a small coffee house across from the hotel. The people who went in and out greeted one another, read their newspapers, and commented on the day's news. "We thought again," says Gordon, "that Christ would have been more at home in the coffeehouse." [22]

Until that time the idea of interpreting the Christian faith through drama, art, poetry, and discussion sessions in an informal place like a coffeehouse was completely new. The Church of the Saviour called its coffeehouse *Potter's House,* because "your life is to be so yielded to the hand of the Potter that you shall be to those who gather in the Potter's House the bearer of this message, a witness to God's redeeming love in Jesus Christ." [23] During recent years, Potter's House has become one of the most spectacular structures for mission; it has become the show window of the renewal avant-garde, visited by artists, writers, beatniks, scientists, businessmen, and politicians. "In the coffeehouse we had a vision, and in the vision the restaurant and factories and taverns of the city had become the worship halls of the church come of age," writes O'Connor in one of the bulletins of the congregation.

The uniqueness of the Potter's House is that it proved to be transformable into a coffeehouse church. It is not a house church where coffee is served, rather it is a coffeehouse where a congregation gathers. The coffeehouse congregation in Washington, D.C., has worked out a coffeehouse liturgy that looks like this: (1) Preceding the worship service is the "quiet hour," a half-hour of silence from 10:30 until 11:00 A.M. ("For those of us who worship at the 'Potter's House', the half hour of silence preceding our worship is the focal point of our week.") (2) At 10:45 music be-

[22] *Ibid.,* pp. 108-9.
[23] *Ibid.,* p. 122.

gins to play from a tape-recording system. (3) The service begins at 11:00. It is always held by lay persons vividly different from one another: a physicist, a potter, an oceanographer, an actress, a chemist, a city planner, and an executive from the State Department. After the confession and absolution follows the Scripture reading. (4) Spoken meditation. Nobody in the Potter's House speaks any longer of a sermon. Instead, the delivery of the Christian commitment is called "spoken meditation." It lasts between fifteen and twenty minutes. (5) Silent meditation. A fifteen-minute period of silent reflection about what has been heard through the spoken meditation. The first few minutes are completely silent. Then, gradually, the music from the tape recorder grows louder. (6) In the last fifteen minutes of music coffee and rolls are served. Obviously, some participants in the coffeehouse worship service regard the passing of coffee and rolls as a legitimate replacement of the normal eucharistic elements. O'Connor tells in one of the church bulletins that "one person who passed the coffee and the rolls found himself saying silently the words of the Lord's Supper." (7) Discussion period. (8) The congregation then is dismissed at 12:15 after the benediction.

There is no question that the celebration of the Lord's Supper with coffee and rolls as the eucharistic elements is a bold attempt to secularize sacred acts that had their proper place in the sanctuary only. An equally "non-religious" interpretation of the other Protestant sacrament, the baptism, took place in an unusual church that can compete in experimental vigor with the Potter's House in Washington, D.C. What happened in that church?

3. THE SHOPPING CENTER CHURCH. Almost everything in our daily lives underwent either drastic changes or slight evolutions during the years following the Second World War. One of those dear old things we had to give up was the grocery store on the corner. A thrilling story could be written under the title "From the Grocery Store to the Shopping Center." Today, the shopping center is a pro-

found expression of the attempt to integrate a multiplicity of functions, a variety of styles of life, and various types of business into a whole, compounded under one roof.

The magnificent and luxurious shopping centers taking shape before our eyes are modifications of mom and dad's dear old grocery store. While our parents went to a grocery store in order to buy something, we today drive to the shopping center in order to look around or shop around. This has already become a life style, a frame for spending leisure time. A church that wants to be with the people on the market street of the twentieth century will follow that trend. One of those "exodus churches" is *The Church on the Mall* in Philadelphia.[24] In one of more than 100 stores in a suburban shopping center in Philadelphia the Church on the Mall, a merger of three Presbyterian congregations, has its church office, a meeting room for small groups, and a place to meet newcomers. According to the secretary of this 560-square-foot church office, "some people are surprised to find no pews here. Others expect to see books and religious articles." [25]

This congregation, under the leadership of pastor Allan W. Kinlock, has recognized the opportunities of this unusual setting. Adult Sunday-school classes meet at the soda fountain, where the group leader stands behind the counter and the class sits on counter stools, as in one of the snack bars. A class of youngsters gathers around the central fountain in the mall. In the community hall, finally, the whole congregation comes together on Sunday morning for corporate worship.

In the summer of 1966 the minister initiated a new practice of celebrating baptism. Since they had this wonderful huge fountain on the mall, why not use it for baptism? Hence, on a Sunday of that year the congregation followed its pastor from the "sanctuary"—the community room of the shopping mall—to the central fountain. There the worshipers formed a large circle surrounding the pastor, who

[24] See *Presbyterian Life,* November 15, 1967, pp. 8-11.
[25] *Ibid.,* p. 9.

52

was holding the baby over the edge of the fountain. Then he dipped his hand into the water and sprinkled the baby's head. This was the celebration of holy baptism in a secular context. It happened in the marketplace of the twentieth century.

Besides these corporate activities, Mr. Kinloch has started a special ministry aimed at the mall's businessmen. He holds luncheons and other meetings concerned with ethical problems arising in the area of business today. And yet, although this congregation has developed a specialized ministry to the mall, it needed to be distinguished from *functional mission in the shopping center* (which will be dealt with later).

SUMMARY

Three major types of locations for congregational gathering can be distinguished: The high-rise church, homes and public buildings, and commercial buildings.

1. The *high-rise church* proved to be a combination of "sacred" architecture resembling a sanctuary and "profane" architecture bringing about the integration of office or apartment units into a building of that kind.

2. *Homes and public buildings* as meeting places reveal a revival of the age-old house-church idea; the latter has found contemporary modifications that make the home-church structure in the technological society very effective.

3. *Commercial buildings* are in one way or another examples of the fact that, parallel with the change of storefront forms in general, the church has adjusted to the revolution in shopping. Its storefront church types are a result of the compromise with modern styles of living (shopping, spending leisure time).

3
Koinonia Forms

The cry for church renewal is deeply rooted in a crisis of the Christian fellowship idea. The question is whether fellowship is based on coffee and doughnuts, lofty chats, and the search for opportunities to be seen in a new dress, or on a new community spirit. Briefly, Christian social life needs a new foundation in order to revive creative koinonia in the church.

In the subsequent discussion the terms koinonia and fellowship must be viewed in a close relation to the sociological term *Gemeinschaft* (community). The German sociologist Ferdinand Tönnies helped us to recognize the two major types of human existence in social relationships. His famed book *Gemeinschaft und Gesellschaft* [1] proves to be of great value for the discussion of a new approach to Christian fellowship. According to Tönnies "all intimate, private and exclusive living together, so we discover, is understood as life in Gemeinschaft (community). Gesellschaft (society) is public life—it is the world itself. . . . Gemeinschaft is old, Gesellschaft is new as a name as well as phenomenon." [2]

Here, however, is not the proper place to discuss this

[1] Translated and edited under the title *Community and Society* by Charles P. Loomis (East Lansing: Michigan State University Press, 1957).
[2] *Ibid.*, pp. 33-34.

issue in detail. This is left to the sociology of religion. What will be done is to apply the distinction made by Tönnies in a slightly modified manner to the emerging forms of fellowship in the recent movement of church renewal. For the purpose of describing experimental churches adequately in regard to their fellowship or koinonia structure, it is sufficient to say that every single form of Christian fellowship can be attributed to either the *Gemeinschafts*-type (communal type) or the *Gesellschafts*-type (associational type[3]) of fellowship. In both cases the dynamics of social relations in the respective fellowship groups follows its specific law. For the sake of greater clarity in the ensuing discussion it may be helpful to restrict the area of consideration a little more. The following discussion of "communal" and "associational" types of Christian fellowship structures in contemporary church renewal will not deal with the *sociopsychological* process in the relations of members of a group. This would be the task of a sociopsychology of religion. The only thing this study can do is to classify communal and associational forms of Christian fellowship structures, i.e., it will deal only with those structures which are already relatively fixed and no more in progress. Likewise, this study will not deal with the specifics of "ingroup" and "outgroup" relations among the members of a Christian fellowship structure. Instead, four criteria have been developed to describe the various fellowship forms in present church renewal: (1) the degree to which a Christian social group has been institutionalized, (2) the presence or absence of discipline, (3) loyalty and reverence regarding the supreme interest of a group, (4) the numerical size of a group.

Although the following analysis takes into consideration findings of the social sciences it seems more adequate to

[3] The German term *Gesellschaft* is usually translated "society." C. P. Loomis did so in his translation of 1957. However, a previous translation of this book appeared in England under the title *Community and Association* (London: Routledge and Kegan Paul, 1955). My study follows this earlier translation and uses "association" for the German word *Gesellschaft*.

speak of *koinonia* forms rather than of Christian social forms. The introduction of this particular theological term helps to sharpen the word "community," which is used as thoughtlessly as the word "revolution" today. The division of Christian koinonia forms into "communal" and "associational" types reflects the cooperation of sociology and theology. What are the characteristics of these two types of koinonia structures? The *communal type* (*Gemeinschafts*-type) is characterized by very personal relationships among the group members, by the presence of a strong group consciousness, by an articulate willingness to sacrifice personal well-being to the supreme interest of the group, and finally by small membership. The *associational type* (*Gesellschafts*-type) is characterized by a larger number of members, by higher organization and bureaucratization of the social structures, and by less intimate relationships of the group members to one another.

We have proceeded far enough now in the discussion to draw a parallel that is striking. For those who want to understand more in depth the nature of contemporary church renewal, the acquaintance with the German sociologist Ernst Troeltsch is indispensable. A careful comparison between the "community-association" typology developed here for the koinonia forms, and the "sect-church" typology of Troeltsch discloses the following two phenomena in experimental church structures: (1) The age-old struggle between church and sect forms of Christian organizations has found its continuation in our time, however with one important modification—that the dispute now is carried through *within* the church itself. The major criterion for Troeltsch in distinguishing between church and sect was the factor of "worldliness." Nowadays, however, this factor may be replaced by sociological criteria.

(2) And yet, the distinction made by Troeltsch is still valid if the factor of "institutionalization of a Christian koinonia form" is viewed as the touchstone, rather than the factor of worldliness. In other words, the decision as to what fellowship type within the Christian church is

characterized as church- or sect-like will be determined by the degree to which the forms of a group are institutionalized and bureaucratized. The "sect" is no longer the "non-worldly" type; rather, now it is the "non-institutional" type.

The distinction between church and sect cuts across denominations of every size whatsoever, if applied in a different way than Troeltsch did. We discover that contemporary church renewal shows two basic types of koinonia. One is the "communal" type (the sect equivalent); the other is the "associational" type (the church equivalent). Considering all these factors, we can find support for our modified thesis in a quotation from Troeltsch's masterpiece *Social Teachings of the Christian Churches*[4]—if the words "world" and "secular" are replaced by the terms "institition" and "institutional." Troeltsch says:

The church is that type of organization which is overwhelmingly conservative, which to a certain extent accepts the secular order, and dominates the masses; in principle, therefore, it is universal, i.e. it desires to cover the whole life of humanity. The sects, on the other hand, are comparatively small groups; they aspire after personal inward perfection, and they aim at a direct personal fellowship between the members of each group. From the very beginning, therefore, they are forced to organize themselves in small groups and to renounce the idea of dominating the world.[5]

With these considerations in mind, we can better understand the following examples of experimental church structures as the new clue for the understanding of Christian koinonia forms in the twentieth century.

THE COMMUNAL TYPE

1. THE DISCIPLINE COMMUNITY. A small group of Christians in Rochester, New York, called *Ekklesia*, represents a type of structure that was adopted by numerous con-

[4] Translated by Olive Wyon (New York: Harper, 1960).
[5] *Ibid.*, I, 331.

gregations stemming out of the renewal movement after the Second World War. It may be said that the discipline community has provided the ground for some of the most effective renewal projects in the United States. *The Church of the Saviour* in Washington, D.C., is noted throughout the ecumenical movement for its disciplined group life. *The Ecumenical Institute* in Chicago, which calls itself an "order," has designed and tested remarkable new images of the church in the second half of the twentieth century. The *East Harlem Protestant Parish* had for many years a staff of ministers who agreed on a voluntary, self-imposed discipline in theological, operational, and economic matters. This disciplined team of ministers made the congregation effective, so that the East Harlem Parish became the prototype of a contemporary parish. Finally the *Christian Faith and Life Community* in Austin, Texas, became attractive in the eyes of students as a new proper form of religious involvement and commitment on the campus. A participating professor wrote of this experimental community, "From the first, there was visible power within this community of students and staff because of the *discipline*, the common life, and the seriousness of study which characterized its common life. The Christian Faith and Life Community rests upon the conviction that the vocation of the student is thorough-going study." [6]

Ekklesia in Rochester was organized in 1962 when several families expressed their desire to share with one another a genuine fellowship experience.[7] The persons who finally made up the constituency are not affiliated with any other church, and they do not miss the structure of the establishment. Instead, they have their own worship service. They have dismissed preaching and teaching—the former, because preaching does not sufficiently involve the listener; the latter, because the group believes that teaching is not at-

[6] *The Campus Ministry,* ed. by George L. Earnshaw (Valley Forge, Pa: Judson Press, 1964), p. 113.

[7] For data see *The Church Creative,* ed. by Edward Clark, *et al.* (Nashville: Abingdon Press, 1967), p. 65.

tractive for young people and starts with the presupposition
that one always has the proper answer. Instead, *Ekklesia* en-
gages in group discussion following a Scripture lesson.

Yet, the most significant characteristic of this koinonia
group is that it favors forms of *discipline* very highly. *Ekklesia* has organized its structure according to a deeper
understanding of discipline. In a position statement issued
by the small congregation we read: "To the best of our
abilities we will give with joy and thankfulness of our
time, talents, and treasure, and will discipline our time and
energies in favor of the deepest concerns of our lives and
the lives of others." Here a group of Christians came into
existence, the members of which could not stand any longer
the "bla-bla-bla" of the system. What they disliked most
in the institutionalized church was that it did not demand
enough from the members and left them uncommitted. In
Ekklesia, however, they achieved a koinonia form where
commitment and involvement are elementary. *Ekklesia* replaced rigid structures with discipline, and the association
of a tithing church crowd with genuine fellowship.

Discipline—in this case the *inner* structure of church renewal—also enables missionary activities. Loyalty and commitment to the chief goal of the group make mission much
more effective than in churches with large crowds where
the individual is anonymous. *Ekklesia* is working through
its members in city slum zones, in a volunteer program at
the state hospital, with crippled children; and it is sponsor-
ing scholarships for refugee children in Hong Kong and
Negro children at home.

These discipline communities, of which *Ekklesia* is but
one example, are widely spread all over American Protestantism. Colin W. Williams, in his book *Where in the
World?* [8] has a small section on the question, A new monasticism? Indeed, the question arises whether these discipline communities are not a kind of new Protestant
monasticism—monasticism being understood in a demythol-

---

[8] (New York: National Council of Churches, 1963.)

59

ogized sense as a group serving God in disciplinary structures. If this is so, then this modern secularized monasticism might become an important factor as it was for the early church—however, in the direction *to* the world. The signs are already here.

2. TABLE AND DIALOGUE COMMUNITY. *Emmaus House* in New York, at 241 East and 116th Street, calls itself "a center of reconciliation and hospitality." Yet, this is relatively ecclesiastical language for one of the most revolutionary structures in mission recently developed in the United States. Emmaus House is known to everyone who reads *The New York Times* (where news of it has appeared even on the front page[9]) and *Newsweek* magazine.[10] What is behind Emmaus House? Catholic book editor William Birmingham, who every Sunday drives his family in from New Jersey, says that it is "the first time that my family and I have found a completely meaningful form of Christian worship in which all of us can really participate."

The idea of Emmaus House goes back to the year 1959. David Kirk, a priest of the Melkite Byzantine Rite of the Roman Catholic Church, established in that year a house of hospitality, a four-room apartment, where some ten people ate, slept, and found friendship. This kind of socialistic approach was introduced to Kirk by the liberal magazine *Catholic Worker.* Later, in 1966, after the completion of his studies, he went together with Lyle Young, a former Anglican missionary from New Guinea, to East Harlem and opened the Emmaus House. This project stands in a sharp contrast to the overtly structured Catholic Church. "We have no blueprint for this commitment," says Kirk, "everybody has to do his thing. Together, we hope to explore a wide variety of new styles in Christian living."

The walls of the room in Emmaus House where the agape meals and provocative adventures in contemporary liturgy take place are not covered with precious frescoes

[9] January 7, 1968.
[10] November 27, 1967, p. 92.

as in age-old churches of Father Kirk's denomination, but are scribbled over with inscriptions and signatures. Some souls have abreacted their enthusiasm for the new koinonia form with chalk and pencil. One inscription reads, "Preparation for becoming attentive to Christianity does not consist in reading books or in making surveys of world history, but in deeper immersion in existence." This creative community counted twenty-five persons in the fall of 1967, plus a staff of six: three priests, a Protestant layman, and two Catholic laywomen. All hold jobs in secular positions. After work they come together in the Emmaus House for discussions and fellowship, and once a month for a corporate meal (the agape meal). On Sunday they celebrate the Mass. Emmaus House may be called the center of a table and dialogue community with numerous additional house churches as koinonia forms, since the members continue their discussions in their apartments. Emmaus House is a kind of integration center for a dispersed group of committed Christians searching for genuine fellowship.

One Friday night the twenty-five members came together with their "worship leaders" to celebrate the agape meal. Father Kirk opened with this toast: "Shalom! To those working for peace, for mediation in Vietnam, those who are in jail for peace, those are actively demonstrating or not demonstrating."

"Shalom!" continued the Rev. Lyle Young, "To effective justice." "Shalom!" toasted a third clergyman from Australia, "To the Beatles who have helped us in our liturgy." Later the Lord's Prayer was recited jointly. Then the participants passed around two loaves of bread and red wine. The dinner the group had was followed by ice cream and coffee. Father Kirk commented, "We are holding agape meals with the connotations of the Lord's Supper *without specifically taking communion.*"

And yet this "remnant" is not just there to enjoy one another's more or less radical opinion about contemporary Christian existence. They also act. Emmaus House where Father Young and Father Kirk live opens its doors to temporary guests. The staff has welcomed hundreds of visitors—troubled priests, black-power leaders, and poor Puerto Ricans and Negroes from the community. Everybody helps to keep the place going. Father Kirk is teaching theology at Iona College while working at Emmaus House. Once in awhile he gets arrested. The last time this happened he had his teaching interrupted; he was protesting the bombing of the civilian population in Vietnam. Others work in the Fellowship of Reconciliation or are involved in inner-city education. One of the laywomen has opened a "Problem Clinic," which helps people from the neighborhood in coping with problems of urban living. All these services are coordinated by this group of twenty-five inner-city Christians, of whom Father Kirk says, they "come together in order to disperse, (are) open to constant change, flexible, pluralistic, ad-hoc, even dispensable."

The publication of the Emmaus ideas is as effective as the life together. *The Bread Is Rising* is the title of its magazine. It speaks out on current issues of importance. It carries articles on the house church, black power, and the ambiguities of life. Through its ardent style it serves as a constant challenge to the ecclesiastical, social, and political system. Another medium of communicating hospitality and reconciliation is the Sunday night lectures. David Callahan, Hans Hoekendijk, George Webber, William Stringfellow, and many other outstanding persons dedicate their time for free lectures and discussions.

Where is this Emmaus House adventure to go? Father Kirk says, "We bypass a lot of structures. We are seeking a style of life that's real to us." The greatest reward of its existence is that it has created an image of the church in our times different from the Roman Catholic establishment. Viewed from the standpoint of church officials Emmaus House is an underground church. The Roman Catholic Archdiocese of New York officially ignores the group, and Father Kirk narrowly escaped a transfer to the Diocese in Rochester. But this reaction of the ecclesiastical establishment is exactly why Emmaus House came into existence.

There are periods in church history when God uses the mini-structures to force open the crusted macro-structures of the system. Meanwhile Emmaus House runs advertisements like this: "We urgently need sheets, pillowcases, towels, blankets, linens, etc. to carry on the work of hospitality."

3. THE MISSIONARY COMMUNITY. This koinonia form is characterized by an extraordinary strong sense of missionary action in the consciousness of each group. This "consciousness for mission" provides the intentional and structural pillar for such a congregation. A living example is *Christ Church Presbyterian in Burlington, Vermont.* The history of this church began in 1955 when the presbytery in Burlington commissioned the Reverend William H. Hollister to form a congregation. However, the execution of this task took an unexpected direction that the denominational executives had never anticipated. Hollister was supposed to organize a church in such a way that it would be able to support itself after a few years without remaining dependent upon the low-interest loan from the presbytery. But in a twelve-year battle Hollister convinced his congregation and the timid executives that the usual idea of success in America is not appropriate for a revolution of the parish structure. Today these very executives are proud of Hollister, a minister who broke through the stereotypes of church renewal.

First of all, Hollister succeeded in holding up the construction of a sanctuary, although a seven-acre plot of land had already been purchased. He persuaded his congregation which counted 114 members in 1966, that the establishment of a church building needed to be given up for the moment, that the search for a new concept of what the congregation should be in the second half of the twentieth century was of higher priority than just piling up bricks. At this point the question arises: What is the concept of the congregation for the second half of our century?

This question can only be answered in the context of the

dialectic between the imagery of the *residential* and the *itinerant* congregation. Christ Church decided to become the latter.

We believe that God is at work in Burlington. He is in our homes, our jail, our places of work, our courts, our city hall, our slums, our playgrounds, our schools and our churches. . . . He's at work in urban renewal, reapportionment, race relations, and wherever there is social tension. And, we believe, that Christ Church Presbyterian exists in order to join God in His work in Burlington and beyond. To this end, we must boldly set a course of action that will enable us to *be* where he would have us to be, and to *do* there what he would have us do.[11]

When Hollister arrived in Burlington in 1955, he started holding Sunday morning service at a public school auditorium. Later the congregation remodeled a TV-repair shop, which provided the sanctuary from there on. Sunday school rooms were in the basement of that building. The next step in "turning the church inside out" was the organization of seven neighborhood groups that Hollister regarded as the structural framework for membership preparation. These "Firesides," as they were called, were in operation before the church could be formally organized in 1956 with seventy-three charter members. During the subsequent struggle, Christ Church found more and more its identity—a missionary community without a permanent church building, but with the spirit of "God's remnant" and the conviction: "We believe it is . . . the primary job of the church to seek where God is at work and to follow him there in obedient service." [12] Pursuing this philosophy, what is the structure of Christ Church Presbyterian as a missionary community?

As a missionary community is always mobile, the struc-

[11] Grace Ann Goodman, *The Pilgrimage of Christ Church Presbyterian in Burlington, Vermont, 1955-1966* (New York: Board of National Missions, United Presbyterian Church, USA).
[12] *Ibid.,* p. 25.

ture of such a congregation is never at its final state. The history of Christ Church's search for an adaptable form of parish life is also the history of the growth of its missionary consciousness. Three stages can be identified.

From 1955-1963 the first stage was the period of clearing the building question, of finding a theological concept, of intensified studies, of experimentation with several small groups concerned with all kinds of problems, and of designing a new style of worship. By 1963 Christ Church offered the following activities:

1) Three service groups: The *Jail Committee,* in which several men found an appropriate expression of their concern for people in prison. Every other week two to six men spent an hour talking to the prisoners and also to their families. A second group is the *coffeehouse (The Loft),* whose waiters are members of Christ Church. They regard their service as an elementary contribution to mission. Once a month they all meet at "the Loft" to discuss operating details and to do some formal study. The *Lund Group* was formed to answer the question: What can a church group do for unwed mothers, who live in a home "like a jail—a secret place behind a hedge where nobody goes"? Christ Church Women had an answer. They visited with these unfortunate girls in the obstetric section of the hospital to introduce them to the techniques of child delivery; they took them to a museum, counseled them, and provided jobs after they had delivered.

2) The occupational groups: *Doctors and medical students* met biweekly for three months to study ethical questions and human relationships in the medical profession. After that period the group fell apart. Several *businessmen* gathered at a Friday morning breakfast for studies of contemporary theological books and current issues of general interest. Two other groups, one for *teachers* and one for *housewives,* did basically the same. The former group, however, was killed off after a few sessions.

3) The Sunday worship in a former TV shop.

4) Membership classes and other adult study groups from time to time.

5) Church school and youth groups.

The second stage in the development of this restless congregation lasted from 1963-1966. That was when Hollister was invited to participate in the first meeting of the North American study committee on the World Council of Churches' theme "The Missionary Structure of the Congregation." Upon his return to Burlington, he worked on a paper that reflects his new impressions from this ecumenical dialogue. The key sentence of his paper about the future shape of the congregation is, "What happened can be described in many terms, but it was God pushing this world in front of our faces. . . . It may also be that it is the world that will present the situation and the structure in which the church should live out its servant life and towards which the church should look for its direction, since it is there that God's mission is even now being worked out." [13] In the light of this theology of mission a basic restructuring of Christ Church took shape, or rather, Christ Church worked out God's mission through structures that already existed: political parties, city government, community council, civil rights groups, and so on. Hence, the congregation renounced setting up its *own* structures. This was a revolutionary step that shook the foundation of Christ Church. This shift may be demonstrated by one example.

The existing Jail Committee no longer worked out its plans and concerns *within* the context of the congregation, rather it began to volunteer in helping with surveys for the study of penal institutions. The committee members interviewed penal officials and helped to get under way a report on the physical facilities at the county jail.

The approach during the third stage, the period following 1966, may be called a secular theology of mission. A revolutionary model of the congregation for tomorrow was elabo-

[13] *Ibid.*, pp. 27-28.

rated. The *missionary community* began to replace Christ Church. The new proposal carries the symptoms of a vigorous prophetic witness. "It is proposed that the *normative* institutional structure of Christ Church Presbyterian be defined by the pragmatic forms in which the church finds itself in mission. In other words, the Loft (the Coffeehouse), Lund (the group for Unwed Mothers), Jail, Occupational and other mission groups *are* Christ Church Presbyterian. We have only to grant them the freedom to authentically carry out the liturgical functions of service, worship, and study." [14]

The future shape of Christ Church is a break with all existing patterns in every aspect. The corporate Sunday morning service at 10:30 was abandoned. Instead, each mission group in the congregation works out its own style of worship. These mission groups (house churches) also take over the responsibilities for the achievement of their own curricula in teaching adults and children. On the first Sunday of each month there is an all–Christ Church community meeting, called the Festival Day.[15] The purpose of this monthly meeting is to provide the corporate context for communication, strategy, redirection, study, and celebration.

One thing is left to mention—namely, that a congregation like Christ Church, whose minister ran successfully for representative to the state legislature, still refuses to build a sanctuary.

THE ASSOCIATIONAL TYPE

Is church renewal possible in small face-to-face groups only? Can the imagery of a non-permanent congregation be formed by a clandestine "remnant" only? Or does the enthusiasm of experimentation vanish before large and

[14] *Ibid.*, p. 37.
[15] For a description of the Festival Day see *Presbyterian Life*, March 15, 1968, p. 5.

anonymous crowds of churchgoers in the prestige churches? If not, what is the role of those highly structured and institutionalized congregations in contemporary church renewal? Gordon Cosby, minister of the Church of the Saviour in Washington, D.C., which represents the communal type, says about the associational type: "The Holy Spirit is still at work in the old structures. People still get converted in them, and personal growth takes place in them. . . . I, myself, came to know Jesus Christ through the old structures. This reproach has been thrown at me time and again, and it is true." [16]

The church with the associational type of koinonia, which is constituted of people who stick to formal membership and regard their relation to the church in terms of a contract (association), and whose minister wants to renew this crusted complex, needs to choose a different way than the churches with the communal type of koinonia. Associational church people see their greatest chance in an evolution from *within,* instead of a revolution from *outside.* The majority of American churches are associations of worshipers, rather than small groups of the committed, but both types of koinonia forms—the communal and the associational—are important for the business of church renewal. The following example represents many churches that carry on reforms within their own walls. It is chosen because of two factors: (1) Church renewal and integration of black people into the congregation go hand in hand. (2) A church with high membership and a considerable degree of bureaucratization represents the opposite pole in the koinonia frame of reference.

Broadway United Methodist Church in Indianapolis is the largest church in the state of Indiana and one of the exemplary churches in American Methodism. However, this congregation is noted not for its wild and radical experimentation, but for the willingness to renew the church

---

[16] Gordan Cosby, "Not Renewal, but Reformation," *Who's Killing the Church?* ed. by Stephen C. Rose, p. 54.

from within and to transform the present institutional structure through a smooth evolution. With 3,300 members, a budget of $300,000, and five ministers, Broadway United Methodist meets all characteristics of a "bureaucratic" fellowship organization, termed here "association."

The year 1961 was the great touchstone to test the integrity of that congregation. Until then, the Fall Creek area —two and a half miles from the heart of the city—had been an all-white community. Accordingly, Broadway's membership reflected this white ghetto situation. Then in 1961 the first Negro family moved into the Broadway parish. More and more Negro families followed. When the first family arrived, it was received with all kinds of ugly actions on the side of the white community. A can of paint was thrown on the porch, a cross was burned in the yard, a shotgun was fired outside the window, and threats followed over the telephone. The situation got worse when bomb threats arrived in the mail. In that situation the senior minister of Broadway, James Armstrong, acted. He demonstratively visited the troubled family to reassure it of his support. This seemingly unimportant incident was a signal that church renewal had just started at Broadway Methodist church.

The next step was to persuade the congregation to stay in that neighborhood and not to join the majority of the white population in their "exodus mood." [17] A major decision was made when the church started to build a $400,000 education and activity unit. Several members left, but the majority could be convinced to keep their church in that area and stick to it. The Sunday before the extension plan was submitted for approval, the first Negro family was received into membership. This was two years after black newcomers to the community were threatened with bombs. An interesting parallel to the highly experimental churches analyzed in the previous chapter may be drawn here. We

[17] From 1961 through 1966 a substantial change in the population of the Broadway area took place. Today only 30 percent of the people living there are white. This figure was 100 percent in 1961.

say that the shibboleth of their renewal work had been the building question, too, but, in a different way. What for the communal type is the decision to *renounce* a permanent church building, for Broadway United Methodist and for all other associational types in such a neighborhood is the decision to *increase* the capacity of the building program in order to demonstrate the resolution to stay in the area.

The emphasis on a strong preaching program combined with a gradual expansion of the renewal program within the limits of moderate experimentation mark the major characteristics of Broadway's reform. Here are the steps: (1) establishment of study groups in the apartments of Broadway members; (2) apartment-house ministry (which collapsed after a while); (3) a program for boys with focus on recreation and athletics (a similar service was provided for Negro girls); (4) a tutoring program with emphasis upon reading in order to combat the unusually high dropout rate in nearby schools; (5) a thrift shop.

Broadway United Methodist is a classic example of the fact that outstanding leadership sets the criteria for church renewal in an associational type of koinonia. The Reverend James Armstrong has verbally through sermons moved the congregation to renewal. "Renewal through preaching" was and still is the predominant theme of parish life in this church.

SUMMARY

In present church renewal new types of congregations emerge together with specific koinonia forms. Contemporaneously, the traditional koinonia forms undergo drastic changes. The representatives of the former species were called the *communal* type, the latter the *associational* type. Furthermore, it can be demonstrated that the communal koinonia form is no longer confined to the traditional imagery of parish structure, whereas the associational koinonia form strives after a cautious transformation of the present. Revolution and evolution appear as the two methodological poles in experimental church life. Or, in other words, the degree of intimacy among church members and the understanding of koinonia determine the degree of radicalism in the selection of new congregational structures.

4
The Expanded Parish

American churches whose congregations reflect the sociological composition of the area can be counted on the fingers of two hands. But there are countless other churches whose constituency is exclusive, homogeneous, ingrown, clannish, and cliquish. Thus, another rewarding battle-ground in present experimentation is what may be called here the "parish zone." The leading theme of this chapter, therefore, is to try to give an answer to the question: What kind of pattern characterizes the zone of influence of a parish in the community? The term parish zone is introduced here to cope with the problem of terminology. After dealing in previous chapters with parish versatility, locations for congregational gathering, and koinonia forms, the task now is to discuss the geographical expansion of a parish—its hinterland, so to speak.[1] What do we mean when we speak of parish zone?

The Western European Working Group of the Department on Studies in Evangelism of the World Council of Churches has defined a zone:

a territorial area within which most of its population lives and works in a complex network of movement and relationships. It may be characterized by three interdependent forces: con-

[1] Hinterland was orginally the land or region lying behind the coast.

centration, differentiation and mobility. Concentration refers to the growth of huge urban areas; differentiation . . . refers to the several sectors of an individual's life, his different and distinct worlds; mobility refers to the constant movement of the individual between his several worlds. . . . The value of developing zonal structures will be readily appreciated. They can provide the vantage points for a right perspective. On the one hand they are a constant reminder of the different world in which people live. . . . On the other hand, they are symbolic expressions, however partial, of the wholeness of life which is the ultimate purpose of the *missio Dei*.[2]

In the following chapter the attempt will be made to describe the largely different radius of different parish zones. Three major types can be identified.

THE REGIONAL TYPE

In Columbus, Ohio, a conference was held in 1967 by the National Consultation on the Church in Community Life to set up imperatives for action in nonmetropolitan America. The preparatory study [3] has prompted a remarkable proposal for the church in the region. The Study Committee has set itself very high standards for a solution of the predicament. They characterize it thus: "The church has reached the crisis point in its existence. The secular society is building new forms. The church can no longer afford the luxury of the traditional institutional forms. To be traditional in either metropolitan or non-metropolitan America will probably mean that the church will be nonexistent as the redemptive agent in society." [4] According to this report the community life is conducted primarily on three levels: (1) the regional level, (2) the so-called functional economic area, which embraces (3) the local

[2] *The Church for Others*, ed. by the World Council of Churches, Geneva, 1967, p. 32. Also, Thomas Wieser, *Planning for Mission* (New York: National Council of Churches, 1966), pp. 208-14.

[3] *Ecumenical Designs* (New York: National Consultation on the Church in Community Life, National Council of Churches, 1967).

[4] *Ibid.*, p. 6.

level. Here are the proposals made by the Study Group of the Consultation for the church structure of tomorrow.

1. THE CHURCH ON THE REGIONAL LEVEL. What is a region? It is "a socio-economic area in the USA. It may vary from 100-1000 miles in radius around one or more metropolitan centers. Mass communication, travel time, and economic ties make the regional unit an increasingly functional entity." [5] What are the consequences for the structure of the church? The central structure, the Study Group believes, should be a research-planning unit. Accordingly, a Regional Planning Cabinet will serve as the primary executive body for this regional unit. This cabinet, composed of elected clergy and laymen and a staff of professional planners, will be responsible for the development of mission throughout the entire region. The legislative body will be what is called the Regional Judicatory, representing a significant concentration of members who are well informed about the major problems in the region and who are capable of recognizing the priorities of missionary action.

2. THE CHURCH IN THE FUNCTIONAL ECONOMIC AREA AND THE COMMUNITY LEVEL. Each region is made up of a dozen or more Functional Economic Areas. As the study shows "these areas have within their boundaries those institutions and resources necessary to be a relatively independent functional unit. These units offer the greatest promise for the church to perform its mission." [6] The chief concern underlying all proposals is the idea that parish ministries need to be located as near as possible to the centers of activity. Four forms of parish concentrations can be identified:

1) The *dominant city* would house the ecumenical center of the prospective Functional Economic Area. A large church in that city will be used as the "cathedral church" for the area. This building would also be the center for a planning staff similar to the planning cabinet on the regional level.

[5] *Ibid.*, p. 105.
[6] *Ibid.*, p. 106.

The "cathedral school" would also be set up there for the purpose of training laymen in this area (the academy for the area).

2) In *the smaller cities* of the area, parish churches are expected to merge. The units that thereby come into existence will be organized around centers of special responsibility—for example, labor, management, business.

3) In *still smaller cities* (less than 10,000 population) the urban church will contact a congregation in the adjacent rural areas. "Whatever the area, the churches involved would be related in a single administrative unit as one parish congregation operating in several locations." [7]

4) In *still more sparsely populated rural areas* a model would be tested similar to that mentioned under 3. A rural Parish Board would include all ecumenically related churches within a "zone humaine," planning for the ministries needed in that parish zone.

Each of these proposals equals the realization of the imagery of an expanded parish, with the parish zone as the radius of missionary activity.

THE ECCLESIAPOLITAN TYPE

After the predominance of churches on the East coast in the renewal movement during the past twenty years, there are indications that the climax has been reached and that a new star is rising on the West coast. East Harlem Protestant Parish and Church of the Saviour in Washington, D.C., hitherto determined to a great deal the pace and extent of the renewal movement. For a decade and longer, ministers and laymen all around the country regarded these two models as the final revelation of the reform movement. Recently, however, this assumption has been challenged. A Western congregation in San Francisco has developed a new style of parish work that may push the door open to a new area of urban church work in general. Because

[7] *Ibid.*, pp. 128-29.

of this novelty, a new term is needed for a church that regards the whole city as its parish. The word "ecclesiapolitan" may be chosen in order to identify this type adequately.

Ecclesiapolitan is a composition of the Latin word *ecclesia*, which means church, and the Greek *polis*, which is translated city. An ecclesiapolitan type of church, therefore, develops mission to every level of urban living and is constantly concerned with the problems with which the citizenship of an urban region is wrestling. The ecclesiapolitan church does not pursue the traditional and narrow concept of neighborhood service only. Instead, the horizon of mission has broadened, and the whole city has become the "parish zone." The ecclesiapolitan church feels responsible for the major events of a city and the major trends of life therein. Accordingly, the parish zone here is the range of metropolitan life. Regarding this type, we discover also the first-fruits of a new social-ethical concept of parish work. The ecclesiapolitan church is the "church for others," the church for the citizenship, the church for the city. This implies new imperatives for ethics, as will be shown later in the account. In a recent WCC paper, the Western European Working Group stated: "A typical zone would be a city with its surrounding fringe towns—an area produced by, and caught up in, the forces of concentration, differentiation and mobility. . . . The zone may be said to have replaced the parish as the geographical area which comes near to integrating the different contexts of everyday living." [8] In this statement the major characteristics of the ecclesiapolitan church are already anticipated.

Glide Memorial Methodist Church in San Francisco is, according to *Time* magazine, probably the nation's most successful and adventurous mission church.[9] The current ecclesiapolitan character of that church is alluded to in the charter of the Glide Foundation to which Glide Memorial belongs. The purpose of Glide's being in San Francisco

[8] Wieser, *Planning for Mission*, p. 210.
[9] October 20, 1967, p. 88.

is "to forward Protestant Christianity in the city. . . . In a thousand ways, Glide says the city belongs to God—and all who dwell therein. God is at work in the events of the city—and God speaks to the city's people through those events." The question arises, What kind of structures and organization are found in a church that has spread its parish zone all over San Francisco?

Glide's church building, a pink sandstone construction, is located on the edge of San Francisco's tenderloin district, a part of the city where prostitution and crime have become a life style for a good many people. Glide Memorial's parish program, accordingly, responds to the specific problems of San Francisco.

Since 1967 Glide has had a new vehicle to carry on its missionary work. Many people at Glide felt that the traditional structure had become largely irrelevant to the special characteristics of San Francisco. Hence, instead of formal church committees, every other Sunday after the worship service the Glide Community Meeting takes place. It is an open meeting led by co-chairmen—one from the ministerial staff, the other a layman. The leading question of Glide's Community Meeting is, What is happening in the world today that we as a congregation of committed people should be responsible to?

As far as the structure of the congregation is concerned, the emphasis is placed on *task forces* rather than on permanent committees. In practice this means that the Community Meeting appoints a special task force, which deals immediately with a specific problem of San Francisco. After the task force—a kind of guerilla troup commissioned to carry on mission in metropolis—has reached its tactical goal, it is dissolved so that its participants are free for new assignments. The uniqueness of this structure is the permanent alertness of Glide Memorial for urban mission through its Community Meeting and task forces. As one of the staff members commented, "We specialize in flexibility"—which means that the entire structure of this congregation is tuned to specific tasks in the urban region.

In May, 1967, the "Black People's Free Store" opened its doors. This storefront, which distributes household goods to the ghetto poor, is sponsored by Glide Memorial. Everybody, regardless of color, gets there what he needs. But this store, which gives away worn clothes and used furniture free, has become also a location where the poor person comes and talks about the brokenness of his life and finds somebody who is willing to listen. The black social worker who is in charge of that store is proud of his twofold function. He distributes things and counsels the poor. The Black People's Free Store has become a center of reconciliation in the ghetto of San Francisco.

One of the boldest projects was to support action for homosexuals several years ago. It is estimated that 80,000 out of San Francisco's 800,000 people are homosexuals. Initially, the Glide Foundation approached this problem with a retreat for churchmen and homosexuals. As a result of that retreat, the Council on Religion and the Homosexual was formed. In the following year, the Council sponsored a fund-raising ball, which about six hundred persons attended. A scandal occurred when police raided the ball, arrested several persons, and took pictures from participants. A police charge was turned down later by a court. Because of this noisy crusade against the indifference of many San Franciscans toward the problem of homosexuality, one newspaper said that "San Francisco's silent war on homosexuals is being forced into the open."

The majority of the board members of the Council on Religion and the Homosexual are homosexuals themselves. A chief goal of this council is, according to its charter, "to promote a continuing dialogue between religious communities, and in endeavoring to understand better the broad spectrum of variation between human sexuality." The research done by the council in this field yielded enough material to provide people who are interested in this problem with background information. Again, this example shows that Glide Memorial, as an ecclesiapolitan type of church,

78

is deeply committed to finding a solution to a city-wide predicament.

From the standpoint of traditional ethics the engagement of Glide in the race problem may be unjustifiable. Yet, for a church that holds that the complexity of life situations decides which ethics to use, the criteria for acting right or wrong are set by the circumstances. Glide's staff (four members are white, one is a Negro) got word in the summer of 1966 of a riot plan in San Francisco's Hunter's Point district. Glide's plan was to hire ghetto leaders in order to quell the racial tension. Hence, $1,000 was given to Youth for Service, an organization of former ghetto gang leaders. They, in turn, hired individuals at $15 a day who helped to cool the tempers of rioters. "We have to come to grips with the world the way it is," says the Reverend Cecil Williams, the Negro on Glide's staff. "If we hide, deny or refuse to engage and be reborn into this new kind of world, then in fact we refuse to participate in God's work." As a result of this action the riot was quelled before it started.

Halfway House, a rehabilitation center for persons recovering from mental illness, is another city-wide project initiated by Glide Memorial. A Glide staff member was one of the first to recognize the need for a Halfway House in San Francisco. He also found a house geared to this service. Afterwards the building was turned over to San Francisco Methodist Mission, which with another church now finances the house. The mental care program, however, is administered and financed by Glide. In this case Glide Memorial acted as a catalyst, an agency that monitored the needs of the city community and developed a kind of missionary instinct for the priorities, and, above all, urged action for pooling resources other than the church's.

Finally, the criteria in San Francisco to decide whether Glide Memorial is really ecclesiapolitan is the question, What is that church doing for the hippies and for the protest generation in general? First of all, Glide is engaged in the solution of problems arising in the youth colony of San Francisco on many levels. Outside its own congregation it sponsors not only new, but also radical ministries. One such was a ministry on the University of California campus in Berkeley, whose chaplain was an ardent supporter of the Free Speech Movement. Glide is also involved in coffeehouse projects in which it helps to provide a platform for Fascists, Communists, and black power militants. More recently, this church backed efforts to set up a halfway house for runaways, the Huckleberry House.[10] Furthermore, Glide initiated an art gallery and a theater where Harold Ehrensperger, a retired professor of religious drama, gives advice and artistic guidance. Also, of course, Glide is concerned with the problems of the "love generation" in the Haight-Ashbury district. As an ecclesiapolitan church, it opened its facilities for multi-media happenings and for free dinners on Thursday nights. And yet, the most exciting encounter with the young generation is the experimental worship service.

The Reverend Cecil Williams, thirty-eight-year-old Texas-born Negro, is famed for his dynamic and unconventional preaching. At a jazz worship service, attended by several hippies, he began his sermon on one October Sunday by wishing everyone "Merry Christmas." The astonished congregation heard him then say: "It's Christmas today, because life comes as a gift." Then he picked up a colored paper sack, which he said was his "psychedelic" bag. He pulled out of it a framed portrait of himself, hung it around his neck, and announced: "I am too concerned with myself. So I carry my hang-up with me, baby. Two thousand years ago, a man said, 'Look, man, you can be free—you don't have to have that hang-up.'" Recently Glide Memorial has also opened all its doors to hippies. In January, 1968, the staff gave permission for hippies to use Glide's Chapel. There, the flower children gathered for "The Free Church of the Free Communion." One of the first things was that some fellows painted the chapel walls and prepared the

[10] *Together,* December, 1967, pp. 52-56.

place for a religious rite according to their own ideas of worship.[11] Again, with this unusual kind of freedom which Glide grants the restless youth of San Francisco, this church proves its ecclesiapolitan character.

There are indications of a new style in urban Protestantism, forwarded by a church whose pulpit is open to Saul Alinsky, whose chapel becomes the arena for tribal rites in hippie manner, and whose minister for youth uttered with regard to the church program as a whole: "The only thing the church has to say is *Yes* to man. *Yes,* you are accepted even if you are unacceptable. This is the key to the kingdom. We say *Yes* to people whether it's through the Black Man's Free Store or the Flower Children's Art bag or happenings in the park."

THE SECTOR TYPE

After the regional and ecclesiapolitan type, the next parish zone to be analyzed is the sector type. The distinguishing mark here is that the church has expressed willingness to exercise responsibility in a certain geographical area strictly defined. The parish zone of a sector-type church is smaller than the regional or ecclesiapolitan, but larger than the plain neighborhood type. What should be the structure of a church in such an area that claims to serve a relatively large district?

Gibson Winter made some proposals concerning such a parish zone. He regards the introduction of this kind of parish zone into the somewhat stalemated discussion on church renewal as a possibility for improvement in the relationship between inner city and suburban churches. He proposes "to stake out an area of Christian responsibility from the outer edge of the city to the heart of the inner city along a major line of access or freeway." [12] Winter views this cross section of the metropolis—as he

[11] *Newsweek,* February 19, 1968, p. 58.
[12] *The Suburban Captivity of the Churches* (Garden City, N. Y.: Doubleday, 1961), p. 144.

calls it elsewhere—as the basic unit of ministry and the minimal unit of the church. Parish work in such a sector, according to Winter, would expand its sphere of responsibility to outside the residential area, but its minimal space would embrace the whole sector of metropolitan life. Winter specifies this idea when he proposes the basic structure of the sector-type church.

Strategically located cathedral-type churches could equally well serve the worship needs of whole areas of communities with modern means of transportation and access. The churches are operating as though the bus, car, and train did not exist; moreover, the "edifice complex" in the suburbs expresses interest in status rather than worship. A suburb or local community could operate with a chaplaincy from an office and employ an educational unit. This unit could have a chapel for special services, but the principal worship for the fellowship of households would take place in the central church from which the local chaplaincy emanated. Several large churches could provide centers of worship for a whole sector of the metropolis; moreover, local buildings could then be designed to meet the particular needs of different areas.[13]

As is the case with all proposals, only a test in rough reality can prove whether this proposal is operable. Meanwhile, some churches working together in so-called larger parishes or cooperative ministries have carried on an experimental service in sectors smaller than the unit Winter has in mind, yet larger than the ordinary parish zone of the neighborhood church. These cooperative ministries or larger parishes[14] show yet another characteristic that is important to know. Besides the responsibility they exercise in a specific *geographical* area, the parish zone, they also show a highly sophisticated *cooperative* working method, since several single congregations are formed into one unit,

[13] *Ibid.*, p. 148.
[14] A good survey of the parish movement in the USA is given by Richard E. Moore and Duane L. Day, *Urban Church Breakthrough* (New York: Harper, 1966), pp. 133-42.

the larger parish. This latter aspect will be discussed later.[15]
Here we are only concerned with the geographical factor,
the parish zone of a sector-type church.

In St. Louis West a remarkable initiative was taken in
1961. A study group of pastors and laymen, led by the
conviction "Together we stand, divided we fail," came to
the conclusion that only ecumenical cooperation between
churches of the West district could give back self-esteem
and self-confidence to the people of the area. All churches
within the geographic boundaries of Taylor, Lindell, Easton,
and the St. Louis city limits on the west were summoned to
join for concerted missionary action. "No one church is in
a position to begin to perform the over-all ministry of service, compassion and outreach needed in the area, if it
tries to go alone. The community is confused by scattered
and seemingly competitive efforts by different denominational groups. Our integrity as the body of Christ is at
stake wherever we refuse to provide a united witness when
it is possible." [16] As the result of an action of missionary
urgency the *West St. Louis Ecumenical Parish* came into
existence.

By summer, 1967, thirteen churches of eight denominations had given official approval to the parish constitution
and had become active members of the group ministry.
Other congregations have participated without giving official approval. The first parish assembly was held in 1961,
and a constitution was worked out. Two basic principles
underlie participation in the parish: (1) equal representa-
tion and participation of laymen and clergy, and (2) reten-
tion by each participating church of its own identity and
the option of participating or not participating in a particular parish activity. "When the parish takes a stand in a
matter of overall concern, the churches in the parish in
agreement with that position are listed." [17]

[15] See pp. 115-28.
[16] From a leaflet of the parish.
[17] From the Constitution.

According to the constitution the West St. Louis Ecumenical Parish has two gubernatorial bodies:

1. The parish assembly. This is the representative body that governs the parish and is composed of delegates from each member church. Each church[18] may designate four representatives to the parish assembly, which holds regular meetings every other month. Besides churches, Christian organizations operating in the west end of St. Louis are also eligible for membership in the parish assembly, which has jurisdiction over all policies, programs, and activities of the parish.

2. The parish board. Elected by the parish assembly, it includes in its membership the officers and department chairmen of the assembly. These departments are: Christian education, worship, evangelism, pastoral service, research, and planning and finance. As the executive committee of the parish assembly, it gathers monthly. Sections 5-7 of the constitution say: "The board shall study the needs of the parish area and make recommendations to the assembly. . . . The board shall give leadership in establishing a common discipline of study and prayer for the parish . . . the board shall have liaison responsibility with community and city agencies, social service bodies, denominational and ecumenical groups."

This structure, which is a *parish* in geographical aspects and a *group ministry* in terms of organization, has successfully served an area in the past six years in which approximately ten thousand people belong to the participating thirteen churches. In that sector of St. Louis a sense of responsibility was formed that would have been unthinkable without the design of a parish zone covering a strictly limited geographical area.

For the sake of completeness a fourth type of parish zone needs to be mentioned—the neighborhood type. How-

---

[18] According to II, 2 of the Constitution "each participating body retains its own identity and autonomy in internal affairs, but will seek to cooperate in any united strategy agreed to by the parish."

ever, since it represents the ordinary setting for the American parish zone, we will not consider it here.[19]

SUMMARY

Three modifications of the parish zone can be identified—the regional, the ecclesiapolitan, and the sector type. The *regional* type reflects structurally the growing importance of zoning and planning. It can shed new light on the chronic isolation of urban and rural church life. The *ecclesiapolitan* type may well be the beginning of a new style of urban church work. This model brings the importance of the whole city as the basic unit of church work into the general consciousness. The *sector* type, although it is nothing more than the introduction of the parish system generally used in American high churches and European Protestantism, was nevertheless developed into a new instrument of cooperation between several congregations. This result reveals a major trend in the organizational emphasis of American Protestantism. Larger geographical units are more and more considered as the basic units for future church work.

[19] Manfred Stanley, "Church Adaptation to Urban Social Change: A Typology of Protestant City Congregations," *Journal for the Scientific Study of Religion,* Fall, 1962, pp. 64-73.

5
Forms of Parochial Ministry

ORIENTATION OF FUNCTION

Present literature on church renewal too often uses the term "ministry" without specifying its connotation. But there is a difference, for example, between the night ministry and a parish program for the Spanish-speaking people. Certainly in both cases ministry means a service originating in the church. Yet—and this point needs to be emphasized —the structure and methods of both types of ministry are fundamentally different. The outworn use of the word ministry was one of the reasons why this book was written and why it was subdivided into two parts. All specialized ministries, to which the night ministry belongs, might be better called *functional (nonparochial) mission.*[1] Likewise, all service by the church performed by the congregation, not by an individual, should be called *parochial ministry.* Congregational structures and functional (nonparochial) mission are the two elements in current church renewal that need to be identified and kept apart.

This chapter will deal with the parochial ministry in contrast to functional mission. Within this parochial ministry, which is carried on collectively by the congregation as a whole, there are *orientation* and *strategy* factors of function. We will discuss in chapters 5 and 6 the *functions*

[1] For an explanation of this term, see p. 131.

of the congregation, whereas chapters 1 through 4 treated the *structure* of the congregation in various aspects. The orientation aspect of function provides an answer to the question: What is the basic philosophical orientation of parish work? The strategy aspect of function, on the other hand, answers the question: What are the means a congregation uses to accomplish an effective ministry? Although distinguished sharply from each other, both will appear together in the subsequent illustrations in order to retain a character of wholeness that each congregation shows, despite theoretical distinctions.

1. PERSONALITY-FOCAL. This term signifies a deep and thoroughgoing concern with spiritual powers, with the rediscovery of the Holy Spirit as a catalyst for the entire parish work. This personality-focal type of orientation may be distinguished further: (a) the edification of the congregation through the spiritual experience of a new community life (koinonia); (b) the edification of the congregation through instruction (didache). Teaching here ranks higher than devotional experience.

First United Methodist Church in Germantown, Pennsylvania, is one of those congregations for which I Thessalonians 1:7-8 could have been written. It has experienced renewal of the parish through renewal by the spirit. This was the starting point of a church that was occupied primarily with itself, when in 1961 Robert Raines was called to serve First Methodist Church. In that very year his book *New Life in the Church* was published. It contains something like the blueprint of Raines's later strategy at that church. One passage especially in that book anticipates the Germantown style: "The church must prepare her people for a lifetime of growth. With one hand the church reaches out to awaken persons to decision for Christ; with the other hand the church guides persons to grow up in every way into Christ. The church is both evangelist and educator, both obstetrician and pediatrician, helping deliver those newly born in

Christ and nurturing them from infancy to maturity in Christ." [2]

The word "koinonia" played an overt role in the reform work of Robert Raines in Germantown. The idea was to seek the structure appropriate to the sovereignty of the spirit. Raines found its form in what he called the koinonia group. Combined with the formation of koinonia groups was a rigorous membership training, which, however, was not as rigorous as Church of the Saviour in Washington, D.C., requires. With three elements in mind—the supremacy of spiritual life, the training of committed members, and the organization of the parish life in koinonia groups—First Methodist Church was transformed into a living adventure of faith.

The emphasis in this congregation upon koinonia is so great that the entire conduct of church life appears as one huge koinonia group mapped into several small cell-group structures. No more than twelve to fifteen persons make up one of these small groups. Raines has said in reference to these small groups within the context of the whole parish life:

Conversation takes place in *koinonia*. . . . There cannot be real firsthand *koinonia* among hundreds of people. The best evidence of this is the fact that hundreds of people in a given local church can worship faithfully for years without any appreciable change in quality of commitment or direction in life. Many of the same people, exposed to a breath or taste of *koinonia* in some small group, begin to change in a matter of months.[3]

This spirit of koinonia breathes through all kinds of programs in Germantown—the teen-age canteen, the membership classes, the ministry to those racially discriminated against, the extensive work with the community leaders or the Covenant House. This latter project proves that a church with an articulate devotional life can be strong

[2] (New York: Harper, 1961), p. 48.
[3] *Ibid.*, p. 71.

in the achievement of mission as well. Covenant House grew out of a koinonia group meeting in 1964. This group, composed of ten people who were members of First Methodist Church, studied Ephesians. One participant remembers: "Paul was inspiring us, disturbing us, pushing us to do something. . . . What *was* our calling? A response came more quickly than any of us had anticipated." [4]

Brinkhurst Street in Pittsburgh runs through one of the low-income housing areas where 60 percent of the population are nonwhite. The small group bought a house there with borrowed money and called it *Covenant House*. The work they carried on there was to contribute to a community remodeling program. Soon the children from the neighborhood came and enjoyed themselves during a structured time of leisure and recreation. In addition a tutoring program was set up, and a medical care service was offered. The response was overwhelming. Support came in for the nondenominational Covenant House from Baptists, Presbyterians, Methodists, Jews, atheists, city planners, businessmen, lawyers, housewives, and retired people. This house of reconciliation received in its first year of operation $5,000 in gifts. The spirit of koinonia had turned the church inside out.

A modification of the devotional type of orientation is that fellowship structure in which the emphasis lies on *instruction* rather than on the experience of koinonia. However, this does not mean that these two forms exclude each other. As one minister in Dallas puts it: "Adult education means the courage to search and the desire for larger and deeper concepts of faith." According to this concept, a church in Dallas has operated very successfully and has gained a nationwide reputation.

Northaven Methodist Church in Dallas was all at once the center of attention when its minister, William A. Holmes, preached a prophetic sermon on the Sunday after

---

[4] Joan Hemenway, "Covenant House in Philadelphia," *Christian Century*, October 27, 1965, p. 1316.

President John F. Kennedy's assassination. His critical remarks about Dallas created a local furor that made it necessary to give him police protection for some time. This dynamic minister moved his congregation by means of a demanding and exciting preaching program. On Holmes's side, however, there was often complaint about the theological ignorance of the congregation. As a matter of fact, he asked his official board to appoint a committee to search for ways to overcome this problem. It proposed some months later a "community dialogue program," which is offered twice a year, each period eight weeks in length. Here is the curriculum:

Sessions 1 and 2: "The Question of God" was the general topic for the first two evenings. The first session dealt with the question: What is faith? Required was some reading from an article H. Richard Niebuhr wrote in *motive*, "The Nature and Existence of God." The general topic for the second session was "Who is God?" Rudolf Bultmann's essay "The Crisis in Belief" from his collected essays was the focal material for study.

Session 3: "The Question of Christ." Basic reading was Paul Tillich's sermon "You Are Accepted" from the collection of sermons *The Shaking of the Foundations*.

Session 4: General Topic: "The Question of the Holy Spirit." Required reading here was one chapter "The Event and the Story" from John Knox's *On the Meaning of Christ*.

The succeeding two sessions were devoted to the discussion of basic problems of Christian ethics.

Session 5: General topic: "The Courage to Affirm the World." For reading material the chapter "Christ, Reality and God" from Bonhoeffer's *Ethics* was chosen.

Session 6: General topic: "The Courage to Be Responsible." Again a chapter ("Freedom") from Bonhoeffer's *Ethics* undergirded the study.

The final two evenings were devoted to the problem of unbelief.

Session 7: General topic: "The Escape in Illusion."

Background reading here was Part One of Kierkegaard's *Sickness unto Death.*

Session 8: General topic: "The Escape in Defiance," with reading from Part Two of Kierkegaard's masterpiece.

There is no doubt that such a curriculum would honor any academic institution. However—and this is a great surprise—nobody in the congregation got the idea that he would flunk the course because of its demanding stress. On the contrary. The courage of Mr. Holmes in introducing members of his church to new frontiers in theology was rewarded by a growing interest in more courses in the future.

As a result of this emphasis on instruction the whole structure of Northaven Methodist Church was affected. By 1965 more than 350 members of Northaven had completed that curriculum. In the meantime, the official board had voted to make such a completion mandatory for membership on the board, for teaching in the church school, and for study leadership in the women's society.

After this preparatory work the next step could be taken. Northaven initiated an annual theological lectureship that surpassed any expectation of what the fire of renewal in one single congregation can ignite. The first lecturer was the late Paul Tillich. When he spoke in 1964 in Dallas, he attracted each evening more than 1,000 people, although Northaven's membership then was 550. The lecturer the following year came from England—the Bishop of Woolwich, J. A. T. Robinson. All these efforts to bring prominent theologians to the congregation, and the conviction that the theological ignorance of the church members needed to be challenged through a demanding teaching program, has made Northaven United Methodist perhaps the most enlightened church in Dallas.

2. SOCIOPOLITICAL. What is the sociopolitical orientation of the parish ministry? It is the kind of parish work that exposes the congregation to the social and political happenings in the parish zone for which it is responsible. If

we think for a moment in terms of "contemplative" and "action-oriented" church work, then all churches that fulfill the categories of the devotional and instructional type may be called the *contemplative* type of parish ministry. The sociopolitical type may be identified as *action-oriented* parish ministry. The talk about the catalytic function of the congregation, or the congregation that is where the action is, expresses a concept of mission that is sociopolitical.

The unrest among liberals—clergymen and laymen alike —about the church's lack of concern for the sociopolitical tasks in society has resulted in a deep desire for something like a grass-roots church. Those who believe they can no longer support churches that do not express social commitment by actions, advocate the church turned inside out. Probably the best illustration of this type is the East Harlem Protestant Parish, not in its structure but in its orientation. Many congregations tried to imitate its style, yet only a few could record some success. One of those successful congregations—which, to be sure, did not simply imitate East Harlem's style, but picked up the major concern of that parish to be alert for sociopolitical operations—was a small group in Indianapolis.

Church in the World in Indianapolis was the product of discontent with the present ecclesiastical pattern and the desire for more action in the church. It came into existence in the fall of 1967 when students, ministers, and professors —all of whom were connected with Christian Theological Seminary, Indianapolis, Indiana—held the constitutive meeting of what was later called Church in the World. Another, more profane, term was "the Sack-Lunch Church," a term referring to the custom of the participants, who used to meet between twelve and two o'clock on Sunday afternoon. Everybody brought his own lunch, which served as the elements of the Lord's Supper. This small group of some fifteen people is by no means exemplary for a church with sociopolitical orientation, yet it provides a good illustration of how churches of that type operate.

The group intended to meet regularly twice a month for

studies and the "celebration of life" in worship. Besides elementary questions of the Christian faith, emphasis was laid upon the study of community needs in and around the city of Indianapolis. During the first three months the Church in the World expressed its strong sociopolitical concern on three occasions.

1) Once in awhile the group, which had no church building of its own, met in a social service center—the Broadway Christian Center of Indianapolis—to support its neighborhood program through the payment of rent for its meeting place.

2) A spontaneous action was started when the group got information in the fall of 1967 that the Negro mayoral candidate in Gary, Indiana, needed financial support for his campaign against the white power structure in that city. Gary later became one of the few American cities with a Negro mayor. Mr. Hatcher's success in the election was greeted with deep satisfaction by the members of the Church in the World.

3) An original idea was the trip of Church in the World members to Chicago to express their concern with the developments in the 1968 presidential election campaign. What happened in Chicago was a kind of "political liturgy." Instead of holding a regular meeting in the dormitory of the seminary, the church members drove to Chicago, where they helped to start the "McCarthy for President Movement." As participants in a political rally the group celebrated its "logical" worship service (Romans 12:1-2) by supporting the peace candidate, McCarthy.

This action emphasis is one aspect. Another is the regular gathering for study and communion service. Prayer, brief meditation, and the summoning for community action are the *verbal* elements. The improvised communion service is the *action* element, action being understood as anticipated in the celebration of the Lord's Supper. One student passes a loaf of bread after having said the benediction over the element. Then everybody takes for himself some wine from the following jug. Needless to say, the anti-institutional character of the Church in the World did not allow the appointment of a minister to serve the group.

3. ARTISTIC-CULTURAL. To proclaim the gospel among artists requires a revolution in the selection of missionary methods. How can this be done most effectively?

First of all, the specific character of the artistic profession puts its stamp on every form of Christian witness in this area of life. The proportionate lack of structure in this vocation requires adequate forms of mission. The challenge for the church is so great that a minister fails before he begins if he is not capable of deploying a rich variety of missionary methods. In this field of mission, to be sure, not the most scholarly theologians operate, but the most original ones. Because of the unconventional life style in artistic quarters like Greenwich Village, the church in its mission stands or falls with the skillfulness of its ministers in the effort to adjust to the world of the artist. Theologically, a correlation point needs to be found; structurally, the church is asked to use the cultural media of communication that those professions use. In other words, the church has to interpret the cultural symbols of the artistic environment in terms of mission. One of the possibilities is drama. The following example tries to illustrate how parish work makes use of drama in order to minister to artists. First, two factors need to be mentioned that characterize parish work in this context.

1) Functional mission among artists usually is performed by a parish rather than a specialized minister alone. The reason for the collective character of this type of mission is that only the congregation can easily provide space for art exhibitions and theater.

2) Functional mission among artists is the only type of mission at all that appeals to the recipient in the totality of his work and life functions. A separation of work and leisure in the art profession is impossible, artificial. Hence, experimental ministry among artists needs to be seen as one of the most universal functions of the church.

94

This universality of missionary activity implies a great variety of experimental forms on the part of the church. The scale goes from the Christian coffeehouse, to art exhibitions in the sanctuary, to the performance of drama—religious and profane in character. This present analysis is concerned only with the *performing* mission—i.e., drama in all its variations.

St. Mark's Church in-the-Bowery in New York operates with different elements of the performing-mission type. St. Mark's is Episcopal, the denomination that has achieved pioneering work in religious drama.[5] This parish offers programs in theater, poetry, and film. Its rector, Michael Allen, is well prepared for this kind of parish work. He is a former writer for *Look* magazine and an outspoken advocate of the use of news media to illustrate sermons. One of his church members, at present director of the theater workshop, says, "I had been an atheist all my life. I was converted by Allen working with him." This remark sheds some light on the experimental spirit directing the work at St. Mark's. Why do people get excited about that church?

1) The *theater* project, called Theater Genesis, is primarily for playwriters and actors. Anyone is free to submit a script, which is read by the theater director. The workshop meets one evening a week, and a selected play is read by young actors and later discussed. Some plays that are considered worthy of production are put on by Theater Genesis and are open to the general public. Father Allen wants to appeal with this art program to those people "who are involved in protest by withdrawal." And he adds, "I have no desire to change their views. I am not interested in taking anyone away from pot. I just want their protest activity to be engaged in society. If they have something to say, I don't just get lost."

2) The *poetry* project is set up similarly. One evening a week is devoted to poetry reading by a recognized poet,

[5] Harold Ehrensperger, *Religious Drama: Ends and Means* (Nashville: Abingdon Press, 1962), pp. 172-84.

95

and one evening is an open poetry workshop where anyone is welcome to read his poetry. A poetry magazine called *The World* is put out about once a month.

3) The *film* project allows interested people to work on the actual production of a film. It is run by a knowledgeable film-maker who does not mind working with inexperienced people. The church, in addition, owns extensive film equipment for this work. Fortunately, this art project is partly financed by a federal grant from the Department of Health, Education, and Welfare. The grant is used to maintain a small art staff, to lease a large building, to purchase equipment, and to produce plays.

This is briefly the description of a parish that has devoted much of its activities to the development of an art program. Besides this type, there are already churches that have organized almost their entire programs toward the service of performing mission through art. Two other examples of New York churches may illustrate this. In parish work fully geared to perform mission through theater, two basic forms may be identified. They do not differ fundamentally, but rather are modifications in the deployment of a common concern: (1) liturgical drama, (2) avant-garde theater. Both use dramatic elements, but the liturgical drama is directed more toward religious issues or is used to interpret sacral acts in the liturgy. The latter tries to provide the correlation point for mission in profane theater.

In a 100-year-old church between Ninth and Tenth Avenues in New York, a few blocks off the theater district on Broadway, the rebirth of a congregation took place in 1962. The strength to do it was created simply by the introduction of drama into the parish life. Since that time *St. Clement's Protestant Episcopal Church* has been one of the pioneering churches in performing mission through drama. It is a church whose vicar, the Reverend Eugene A. Monick, says, referring to the use of dramatic elements in worship, "We have Holy Communion each Sunday at 12 noon—which we play with quite a bit, but which we keep central because it keeps us central. Into this we bring all kinds of good secular material—and let it speak for itself within this sacramental context. Scenes from plays, readings, people with something to say—these are the sermons. It's not a unique idea. But the plain fact is that while this kind of revolution is talked about a great deal, it's not often *done*. We do it." [6]

It all started in 1962. Sidney Lanier, a priest of the Episcopal Church, saw the chance for the then nearly dead congregation. With deep sorrow he had watched the decline of parish life at St. Clement's and the growing irrelevance of the Broadway theater as well. Soon his plan was laid out—renewal of both the congregation and the profane theater, each in its own way. Finally, Bishop Donegan from the diocese of New York gave Lanier the permission to start with a "theater mission," with the sanctuary of St. Clement's as the theater place. Hence, this parish in the Time Square area officially got a green light for experimenting with drama, and also added to the various types of new ministries that of the performing mission through drama.

In order to realize this blueprint, the church was exposed to radical renovations. The pews were removed, as well as the high altar, the baldachin, choir furniture, rood screen, confessional, Lady chapel, and side altars. In the sanctuary a large platform was built for performances. The rector's apartment on the third floor served as lighting and sound booth. All this technical equipment was geared to incorporate theatrical performances into the body of the Sunday service. Both theater and church, or better, the church through its dramatically formed worship service, has given new impulses to the parish life.

Indeed, the new start of a near-dead congregation has been of revolutionary vigor. What St. Clement's is doing in terms of experimenting with dramatic elements, theatricalized sermons, and the concept of performing mission is

[6] Sam Tamashiro, "Revolution in a City Parish," *World Outlook* magazine, March, 1967, p. 21.

unprecedented. About 60 percent of the people who used to participate in the Sunday morning service have in one way or another close relations to the world of art. Pursuing the concept, "liturgy is drama . . . and theatre can be and should be revelation," [7] Mr. Monick has consequently turned the entire old-fashioned liturgical setting upside down. "Our point on Sunday morning is," says Monick, "to indicate by our inclusion of dramatic scenes, dance, poetry, political discussion films, etc., that God speaks through men who have vision and creativity and courage." [8] The traditional pillars of the worship service—the sermon and the eucharist—undergo in this process a drastic change.

First the sermon. Churchgoers not acquainted with the style at St. Clement's would be shocked about what happens there during worship service. They would hear only on ten Sundays throughout the year a "real" sermon, i.e., the monologue structure of communication. At. St. Clement's, however, the remaining forty-two Sundays of the year are devoted to the visual and dramatic structure of communication. "Our sermons," Monick explains, "often take the form of the non-homiletic devices. We do not do this indiscriminately. We use our judgment through a program committee, every member of which has a finely honed Christian background and sympathetic understanding of what the Gospel is." [9] How, we ask, does such a "theatricalized" sermon look in practice?

Usually, the procedure is that the dramatized portion is presented at the beginning of the service against the screens placed in front of the altar. Then an actor reads from the pulpit some poetry or literature. On Palm Sunday, 1962, the general theme of the worship service, "Dying We Live," was illustrated by actors rising in their places in the congregation to read letters written by persons in Nazi concentration camps. On another occasion, at the end of the performance the screens were removed and the service

[7] *Ibid.*, p. 23.
[8] *Findings* magazine, October, 1967, p. 5.
[9] *Ibid.*

continued. Mr. Monick in his sermon picked up the points indicated by the dramatic presentation of that day. Scenes from Ibsen's *Brand* served to demonstrate a subtle aspect of the father-son relationship between God and man. The commentary of this dramatic presentation from the pulpit was: "Brand is a fiery evangelist, who represents the worst that can happen to Protestantism when it loses its orientation of salvation by grace."

Another time Mr. Monick opened the service ("We have no choir, only a guitar") by simply saying "Good morning." He then announced that a short play would be given and that the name of that one-act sketch was *The Taxi.* After the play was over, the altar was moved to the center of the stage, and the service proceeded. Since the American Place Theater, a membership theater that has no boxes, has found its domicile at St. Clement's, the congregation sees plays for the first time in its sanctuary that later become attention-getters on Broadway. This was the case with William Alfred's *Hogan's Goat,* which began its life at St. Clement's in October, 1965, and subsequently moved to a theater where it had a long run.

So far we have been concerned with the transformation of the sermon stereotype. What about the eucharist? Ordinarily, there is no service at St. Clement's without both sermon and eucharist. Thus, the later was reinterpreted, too, and enriched with dramatic elements. Monick said, referring to this effort, "People at the eucharist stand up, for the most part as does the priest. We sing Fr. Mitchell's American Folk Mass often—and the protest songs for hymns. . . . We use a whole loaf of Syrian bread, and we come around the altar in a circle to receive. The eucharist becomes a happening." [10] All these things show that at St. Clement's the active (dramatic) connotation of the Christian tradition has surpassed the contemplative dimension. The visual has dominated as a major means of communication. St. Clement's reveals that the word crisis in

[10] *World Outlook,* p. 5.

general and the sermon crisis in particular in Protestantism
("the sermon has diminished in importance at St. Clement's") was met successfully by introducing artistic elements.

This interweaving of drama and liturgy is, according to
the dramatist, a very old element of the Christian tradition;[11] it has merely been rediscovered in our times. Because of the fact that the church has taken dramatic elements into the liturgy after a long historical indifference
towards the arts, the church has become relevant again
for those who can understand an ultimate concern through
the medium of art only.

An article in the *New York Times* about *Judson Memorial Church* in New York began with these words: "There
is no livelier theatre in New York than the Judson Memorial Church." [12] Indeed, what other means can a church
use to "perform" mission in New York's Latin Quarter?
Greenwich Village has become a cosmopolitan spot for
artists and hippies alike. How do you communicate the
Christian faith in this environment without being silenced
at once?

Howard Moody and his associate, Al Carmines, decided
to save the Judson Church from spiritual death by starting
a strong theater program that, they hoped, would give back
relevance to the Bible as a spiritual guide. And, indeed,
they were successful. Following the year 1956, Judson Memorial developed a spectacular mission program through
drama, making use of both liturgical drama and avant-garde
theater. Since we have already dealt in length with the
former, a special emphasis will be put here upon the avant-
garde theater.

"The two great doctrines of Christianity are salvation
and creation. There has been too much concern with the
first. Judson wants to do more about the second," says
associate minister Al Carmines. And he adds, "That was

---

[11] Ehrensperger, *Religious Drama: Ends and Means,* pp. 74-93.
[12] Stanley Kauffman, "Music by Al Carmines," July 3, 1966.

the basis of it all. When I started the theatre in 1961 with
the help of Robert Nichols who's an architect and play-
wright, we had two principles. One, not to do religious
drama. Two, no censoring after acceptance." [13] This concept was elaborated years before Moody and Carmines
came to Judson Memorial. The tragically assassinated
Robert Spike, who became the director for the Commission
on Religion and Race of the NCC after serving at Judson
from 1948-1955, began there with programs in the arts.
When Moody arrived in 1955 as Spike's successor, he laid
the foundation for a broad program in the arts. As a first
step Judson Gallery came into existence.

Later followed what Moody believes was the pioneering
deed in New York as far as the organization of a happening
is concerned. The first happening, with Allan Kaprow, took
place at Judson Memorial. The excitement about the use
of arts in the parish program becomes understandable when
one knows Mr. Moody's philosophy of theater experiments,
i.e., that the present search for new forms and values is the
modern-day equivalent of the old religious search.

The next step in organizing a program of performing
mission was taken in 1961 when the Judson Poet Theater
was formed. From there on the theater was the focal point
of parish life. This, conversely, had implications for the
conduct of the worship service. Moody once said, with reference to a newly developing style of worship,

The theater has affected the style of worship in the church.
But in other ways, too. We threw away the pulpit. We stand
on the floor with the people. There are no pews, only chairs
in a semicircle. People get up and give concerts during worship.
About anything, their poverty, their troubles with doctors, anything. During the prayer of confession we put in things we
think relevant—like war headlines. During the Offertory sometimes there is dance. After all, dance is an offering.[14]

[13] *Ibid.*
[14] *Ibid.*

Lincoln Christian College

101

Besides the liturgical drama, the avant-garde theater, too, was adopted by the art program. In 1961 when Judson started with theater, Lawrence Kornfeld directed its first production, Joel Oppenheimer's *The Great American Desert*. Kornfeld later became resident director of Judson Theater. He and Mr. Carmines, who himself writes music and was successful with some Broadway musicals, have formed what is called the Judson style. Many of the same artists appear in one production after another. One of the best presentations of Judson's theater was Gertrude Stein's *What Happened?* Performed by five dancers—a girl and four men—and a quartet of singers (for which associate Carmines wrote the music), it was totally abstract. It was a "meta-theatrical revelation" as one magazine review put it. One of the actresses said recently, "There is none of the frenzy of the professional theater at Judson, and that is terribly relaxing. It's partly because we don't get paid. . . . You can play all kinds of different parts at Judson. You can really grow as an actor." Other plays were Apolinaire's *The Breasts of Tiresias* and George Dennison's *Vaudeville Skirt*.

Yet another expression in the program of performing mission are the presentations by the Judson Dance Theater, which came into existence in 1962. The Judson dancers dance to jazz accompaniment, to electronic music, to random music from a radio playing on the stage, and to the sound made by furniture. Dances are common during worship service. Altogether, dancing, playing, and celebrating have become elementary issues in the parish life of Judson Memorial. Artists from Greenwich Village have come to appreciate this. Quite a few visitors at the theater of dance performances can be persuaded to participate in the worship service of the church as well. The reason for their coming is that they have noticed the attitude of Mr. Moody and his colleagues, which finds its expression in the fact that artistic and dramatic elements have found their proper place in the worship service.

SUMMARY

We discovered three types of ministries in the orientation aspect of function, orientation here meaning the basic concept of a congregation concerning mission.

1. *Personality-focal.* Here the program of a church concentrates primarily on strengthening the personality through participating in a group or belonging to a congregation. This type of mission tries to address people in their longing for true personality as something that ought to be "built up" by stressing the importance of religion for the growth of one's total spiritual health. Personality-focal ministry does not imply necessarily pietistic practices, but calls for a well-balanced relationship between religion and the growth of personality. Misunderstandings, however, are not totally abolished. Some personality-focal programs do concentrate too much on the "self" instead of the "other."

2. *Sociopolitical.* Quite different from the previous type, this one has proved, however, not to be incompatible with the first. While the personality-focused program has the individual more or less as its objective, the sociopolitical orientation is directed toward the social involvement of Christians in the political, cultural, and economic struggles of our time. Raising one's voice in public affairs is the chief concern, while the growth of personality is of minor concern. Meditation, group dynamics, and theories of personality growth are characteristic of the first type; civic action, organized pressure, and support of the underprivileged of the other.

3. *Artistic-cultural.* This orientation of church work demonstrates an interesting synthesis between the previous types. The parishioner is addressed as a person as well as a potential activist. The use of art in the church is not *l'art pour l'art*. It is a summoning for the engagement of the individual; it is a socializing factor. The use of drama, dance and poetry reaches the individual as a member of a constituency that in its peculiarity can be reached only through these media. Thus the artistic-cultural orientation

of church work is also a valuable contribution to the theme "mission through the communicative arts."

STRATEGY OF FUNCTION

So far we have dealt with the *orientation* aspect of the parish ministry only. It is time now to analyze the *strategy* aspect. While the orientation frame of reference provides contemporary church renewal with the theoretical concept, so to speak, with the ideology of experimentation, the strategy frame of reference compiles methods developed in the achievement of that concept. The subsequent account will introduce four major types of strategy found in the current search for new forms of the congregation.

1. TASK FORCE. This type represents a means of strategy that goes into operation when quick achievement of a specific task becomes necessary. Some theologians speak of "ad hoc" structures when they want to describe a group of committed Christians alert for an assignment in mission. The lifetime of a task force is dependent upon the length of time it takes to achieve a missionary goal. In other words, a task force ceases to exist as soon as the specific task is completed. A task force, one can say, is a guerrilla squadron that attacks the soft-mindedness of society by means of the tenderheartedness of its missionary warriors.

As mentioned above,[15] Glide Memorial Methodist Church in San Francisco has shifted its entire parish structure from permanent working groups to the task force concept. In a bulletin of that congregation it was stated:

There would be a minimum of regular and permanent commissions or committees, with emphasis instead placed upon task forces. Task Force describes a group which would be set up immediately to deal with specific problems and needs. Those persons most interested in a given area would, as a result of their concern, become the task force. Such task forces would exist in structure and in length of time as conditions and the degree of concern dictated. In the Community Meeting [every

[15] Cf. p. 76.

104

two months, and open for the entire Glide Community] specific issues would be voiced and the appropriate consensus and strategy developed. Task Force would work on anything from adult education to police problems in the Tenderloin [a district in downtown San Francisco]. The only limit would be the concern and capabilities of the Glide Community.

The idea of changing the parish structure, leaving the traditional permanent group system behind and turning to the task-force arrangement, provides this congregation with a considerable degree of flexibility. The parish thus is constantly on the move. This might sound revolutionary. And yet, for those who want both elements—the permanent groups and the task forces—the Consultation on Church Union (COCU) approved at the fifth plenary session in Dallas, May 2-5, 1966, a proposal that may be characterized as moderate. According to the documents published after the conference was over,[16] the structure of the local congregation is supposed to look like this:

The basic local units of the united church will be two kinds. One will be *parish-congregations,* organized on the basis of the residence of their members, for worship, witness, education and service. The second will be *task groups* for mission, education and service. There may also be worshipping communities, but organized for specialized functions. These task groups will be made up of persons drawn together by a common vocation in the world or in the Church. All parish-congregations will have general functions in contrast to the task groups which will be focused on one or more limited functions. Each local unit will be obligated to work in ecumenical cooperation, as far as possible, rather than separately.[17]

2. PERMANENT COMMITTEE. The next type of strategy, the permanent committee, is a form that is contrary to the task force structure. By the same token, with these two types we face the old and new concepts of parish work

[16] *Principles of Church Union.* Adopted by the Consultation at its Meeting 1966 (Cincinnati, Ohio: Forward Movement Publications, 1966).

[17] *Ibid.,* pp. 68-69.

in general. The old permanent committee system was—and for many churches still is—based on a very static understanding of parish work. Peer groups meet regularly, cultivate a predominantly theoretical discussion program, and operate for years. The task force, on the other hand, comes into existence if circumstances require quick response on the part of the church. The permanent committee, however, is relatively unaffected by actual events.

Two factors have called into question the supremacy of the old form:

1) After 1948 ecumenical conferences and working groups elaborated new concepts of mission. This new theology of mission (the church as one existing for others) has prepared the church to take more seriously and deal more effectively with social ethics in its everyday life. A task force is always in the service of mission, but the permanent committee is not necessarily so, since it lacks flexibility. "Permanent" means that a group gathers regularly, at a certain time, at a certain place, with the same membership composition, pursuing the same topics over a longer period. In short, the permanent group represents structurally the *discursive* element, the task force the *operational* element in the parish work.

2) Another reason for the rise of the task force concept, and accordingly a diminuation of the permanent committee idea, is the growing influence of conflict as a means to settle social problems. Since the current parish work in areas of conflict is utterly dependent upon cooperation with community leaders, it has become acquainted with all kinds of social action methods, among them the task force structure. The adoption of secular forms of operation has introduced a fruitful unrest into parish work.

3. COMMUNAL PARTICIPATION. As already mentioned, the church today can achieve effective mission only if it enters into cooperation with several organizations and community agencies. Hence, the church once in awhile is asked to cooperate with nonecclesiastical organizations in the pur-

suit of a common task. If a congregation makes its contribution through this kind of action, not autonomously but cooperatively, we speak of communal participation. Following this strategy, the congregation takes part in a major project that neither it, itself, nor another organization, can handle on its own. In most cases the congregation will initiate community action, or it will make its contribution in terms of personnel and money as a part of a concerted action with other agencies.

The Ecumenical Institute in Chicago is a lay training center and a "blood bank" for new ideas in church renewal as well. The staff there has elaborated and tested one of the most genuine concepts of a model geared for participation in community affairs. All considerations and blueprints designed by the staff, which are to be tested and exposed later to the rough reality of Chicago's daily life, take their starting point as a conviction. It is the conviction that the local congregation is the focus in church renewal today and has gained dramatically in importance as the basic unit for mission, despite its despisers. This concept, however, is not generally accepted in theological circles. Many theologians even see the local congregation as outmoded and ineffective as it can be. That the church of the future will have *non*parochial structures is most vigorously presented by Gibson Winter of the Chicago Divinity School.[18] How is the parish model of the Ecumenical Institute constructed so that it can stand the fire of criticism from many sides?

The congregation of the future, the members of the Institute hold, has an inner theological structure and an outer social manifestation of its community concerns. First of all, the inner theological structure:

1) Common worship: The congregation will be a cluster of house churches. However, it is to be a unity subdivided into many cells. The Ecumenical Institute calls the cell group structure "house church." The members of the house

[18] *The New Creation as Metropolis* (New York: Macmillan, 1963), p. 124.

churches will inquire into the importance of worship and liturgical celebration for everyday life. Ordinary meals are regarded as already sacred in character without the need to be especially consecrated. This new understanding of the Lord's Supper is already practiced as part of the training program each weekend when the meals the weekend interns take together are regarded as the celebration of the Lord's Supper.

2) Common study: Each house church will enter into the study of contemporary theology. In addition, a training program will be elaborated for each age level of the house church. Advanced methods of teaching in public education will play a major role in the development of an efficient curriculum for the members of each house church.

3) Common discipline: Each member of the house church is expected to submit his personality to the common goal of the entire community. One staff member of the Ecumenical Institute put it in these words: "We are 20th century people. We are searching what is relevant for our time. We live in a one-story universe, and we know there is no God upstairs. God is a happening. We believe that the individual finds himself, saves himself only through identification with the group. By group we mean the family, the neighborhood, the nation, the world."

4) Common action: Action carried on by the congregation is no mere accessory, rather it is the peak of the parish life. The individual person, the member of the house church, works with his fellow Christians from other house churches in such a way that corporate action becomes imperative. Or in the language of the Ecumenical Institute, "The body must directly act as a unified pressure in bearing witness and establishing justice. This is to say the congregation as a congregation acts." [19] The practical application of this

[19] From the pamphlet "Experimenting with the structures and dynamics of the local congregation," 1963. For a recent assessment of the Ecumenical Institute, see the sarcastic essay by Stephen C. Rose, "The Ecumenical Institute: Ode to a 'Dying Church,'" *Christianity and Crisis*, November 11, 1968, pp. 263-70.

concept was made in the "Fifth City Project." This project was the exploration of the outer social manifestations that the congregations of the future assume in addition to the inner theological structure.

Presupposing the four principles listed—common worship, common study, common discipline, and common action—the parish model to be described next was established.

The *Temple,* a hugh deserted garage, is the place where corporate and "representative" worship takes place. It serves as the coordination center for the congregation as a whole, which is subdivided into numerous house churches. The *Synagogue,* next, serves as a kind of training center where the members of the house churches are trained for social-ethical involvement in concrete mission. The *Guilde,* finally, is composed of small action groups—guerrilla troups, so to speak—for mission in society. These groups carry on the action program of the congregation.

In the fall of 1963 the institute started to experiment with this model. First of all, synagogues were formed that, in terms of structure, are in fact house churches. Each house church is limited to twelve families. In these synagogues lively discussions take place about the form and function of the Temple and the Guilde. The Guildes came into existence in the form of small action groups participating in a community reform program (the Fifth City Project) in the neighborhood of the Ecumenical Institute. This project manifests the willingness on the part of the congregation (which is composed at present of the staff of the Ecumenical Institute and its families) to promote mission in a concrete context.

The explanation of the nature of this project can be found in one of the publications the institute put out: "The name for the Fifth City Community Reformulation Project comes from a typological scheme for classifying the people in the metropolitan area into sub-'cities.' [For example, the second city are people who have decided to return to the city, living in the larger downtown apartment buildings, liberal in orientation but not working structurally for the reformulation of the city.] The Fifth City are people who have decided to pick up the task of reformulating the city in our time." [20]

This Fifth City Project operates with five presuppositions:

1) A community reform program must be conducted in a limited geographical area. A sixteen-block area was chosen. By that time 4,560 people lived in this area. Then, in the fall of 1966, Fifth City territory was divided into five subdivisions called "stakes." Later, this number was increased to ten units. The people of this zone meet weekly for planning and regular house-to-house visitation.

2) Community reform must deal with the deep human problems to be found in this area. In practice the major task is to re-establish a strong self-esteem among the apathetic people in the area.

3) The key to the identity-building phase of community reform is the intentional use of symbols. In connection with what was said under Point 2, this means that the symbols point beyond themselves to pride in being a black person. As a pamphlet put out by the Ecumenical Institute puts it: "They [the symbols] point to pride in community identity. And they point to the conviction of the necessity of assuming responsibility for the lives of the residents themselves and for their neighbors." Those community symbols are the wearing the black beret, the Fifth City emblem (a red wedge shape with blunted tip set on a black circle representing the world), and opening and closing rituals at all public meetings.

4) Community reform must deal with all the critical problems of a community simultaneously. Hence, economic, cultural, and political issues go hand in hand, education being of supreme importance. Besides all that, an extensive leadership training is carried on. For that purpose the stakes are selected as the primary ground where leadership training takes place. While the stake meetings are once

[20] *Image, Journal of the Ecumenical Institute*, No. 4, Summer, 1967.

a week, the "presidium" brings to the table all key stake leaders for planning and policy determination. This presidium gathers monthly.

5) Community reform, finally, must deal with all age levels in the community. During the summer of 1967, the Fifth City Project had twenty-four programs in operation, with the youngest participant being thirty-five days old and the eldest eighty-seven years.

This is, in short, the model for the participation of a congregation (in this case, the community of the Ecumenical Institute staff together with the people from the neighborhood) in community affairs.

4. FUNCTIONAL MISSION. Almost every theological student gets excited about the prospects of his future involvement when he hears or reads something about specialized ministries. An increase of interest in working as a night minister, as a minister to the assembly-line worker, or as a minister to apartment house dwellers has boosted this nonparochial field of church service. By the same token there has been a considerable decrease of willingness to serve in a parochial setting.

The term functional mission[21] signifies every assignment or missionary involvement that is carried on not *corporately* by a congregation, but individually by a clergyman or layman. Functional mission (to minister where people work, live, and spend their leisure time today) to different professions takes place outside the parish zone of influence and requires specialized skill. This is why it is called "nonparochial" ministry. The question arises here, can a congregation carry on functional (nonparochial) mission? Before an answer is tried, the two basic types of ministries today—the parochial and the specialized (or functional)—will be explored more. We have already mentioned differentiation as an important factor underlying the modern style of life, work, and leisure. The present state of our society, indeed, requires flexibility on the part of every

[21] For the explanation of this term, see p. 131.

individual. Accordingly, the church has begun to respond to the social flexibility with a versatile style of mission, so to speak, with distribution of responsibility and competence for each corner of the broad field of mission. As a result the missionary specialist, without whom the proclamation of Jesus Christ in our present technological society is no longer relevant, has gained in importance. The intention to minister functionally is primary here. The elaboration of appropriate methods is secondary and up to the individual person in charge. The reason we have today so many different types of ministries is that the nature of a specialized ministry correlates very closely with the temperament and personality of the person in charge.

Why are parish ministry and functional mission (specialized ministry) distinguished in the present account? The analysis of a number of congregations has shown that church work *within* the congregation (the parish ministry) is less specialized than the work *outside* the parish (the functional mission). To be sure, the ministry among those who are already church members is indispensable. And yet, a congregation is, according to a recent concept, the "congregation in mission"—i.e., its entire structure has to be designed in order to give a direct response to the needs of those people who are *not* members of a Christian fellowship. The Lord has not permitted that a congregation be concerned with itself only.

The traditional nomenclature has described the difference between the two general realms as parochial and nonparochial. Even today it still is a common terminology among reformers and progressive theologians. However, more caution in the use of these terms would be helpful, since this terminology is based upon the *geographical* orientation of the whole issue. Nonparochial, according to this logic, would describe every activity that takes place outside the parish boundaries or the self-imposed zone of influence of a congregation. Yet, these categories can no longer be appropriate to the complexity of the situation. Instead of thinking in geographical categories we should start to describe the problems in *functional* terms. Parochial in this approach would be everything that is carried on in a corporate and relatively *unspecialized* manner by the congregation as a whole. Nonparochial, on the other hand, would be a specialized service to any group of persons outside the congregation carried on by an individual (usually a clergyman) in a highly *specialized* fashion. We return now to the question that was raised before, Can functional mission be carried on by a congregation?

This question can be answered affirmatively. What is more, the congregation will be compelled in the future to accomplish functional mission as a necessary supplementary service, since many parishes are sociologically emasculated. The lack of a representative social cross section among the members of the congregation has added to the loss of functionalism of the church in society. Thus, in order to strengthen and update its membership, a congregation needs to develop functional mission through an extra minister or layman. An assembly-line worker, for instance, will appreciate the healing power of a congregation that is organized on a local basis and that cultivates the spirit of genuine fellowship. Yet, this very worker can be attracted to the idea to join such a community only if a specialized ministry has been set up in the area of his daily work and interests. The functional mission provides connections between him and a community in *his* world, within *his* mode of thought, and deserving *his* trust. Seemingly, we are approaching an era where the missionary specialist recruits the members of a local congregation.

SUMMARY

The discussion of the strategy aspect of function has brought forth four types: task force, permanent committee, communal participation, and functional mission. Each in its part contributes to the nomenclature for the description of specific methods of function. The *task force* was identified as a flexible action group that ceases to exist as soon as the goal of operation is reached. The *permanent committee* —representative of the nonfunctional traditional parish work—as counterpart to the task force, emerges out of the desire to discuss theological issues over a longer period rather than act on the actual occasions and the "happenings" of God in the community. *Communal participation* sees the congregation involved in community tasks together with other organizations. *Functional mission,* finally, responds to the process of differentiation in today's society, and provides specialized methods of social-ethical involvement for current church activities.

6
Forms of Parish Cooperation

The willingness to cooperate between parishes and their officers is the touchstone for the ecumenicity of church renewal. The simple fact that certain means of collaboration were employed has become in many cases the presupposition for a series of successful experiments in other aspects. As long as ministers and board members only talk about the ecumenical movement without taking some decisive steps toward killing the germs of divisiveness in the congregations, the impact upon the local parish will be nil.

Common worship with other churches on Good Friday is not enough, since it reflects but a tradition, a nice custom, rather than an everyday working style. We need to quit with our Sunday ecumenicity and turn to a weekday cooperative spirit that can overcome congregational selfishness. A conference of pastors in St. Louis several years ago coined the right phrase when they became aware in a dialogue that "together we stand, separated we fail." There is no movement of cooperation between the churches in our century that is more widely known and more stimulating than the ecumenical movement. But it has not yet reached the majority of parishes. There is a certain irony in the fact that the cooperation between denominations is more improved than the collaboration between two small country churches of the same denomination, only a mile apart from each other.

COOPERATIVE PARISHES

Included in the analysis of this section are those churches which have adopted traditional patterns of collaboration, hence work together on a nonexperimental level. In order to analyze the whole of church cooperation, a survey of these already institutionalized forms is indispensable before we can move to the experimental new forms.

There are three major possibilities for exercising ecumennicity between churches: (1) Denominational cooperation between Protestant churches of the same denomination; (2) interdenominational cooperation, between Protestant churches of different denominations. (3) Para-denominational or ecumenical cooperation, between Protestant and non-Protestant churches.[1] Besides these general possibilities three specific types of techniques of cooperation may be identified:

1. EXTENDED JURISDICTION. The subject of interest here is variations in the pursuit of administrational and jurisdictional authority.

1) Extended ministry: A larger town church shares its ministry with a smaller rural church. This is a typical example of problems rural churches face today. Because of the increase in the cost of living and the gradual rise of ministerial salaries, more and more country churches will be

---

[1] Three books may be mentioned as prime sources for this theme. One is *Grassroots Ecumenicity,* ed. by Horace S. Sills (Philadelphia: United Church Press, 1967). Sills has collected case studies of local church consolidations. This book discusses the major types of cooperation on pp. 5-10. Another helpful book is Marvin T. Judy, *The Cooperative Parish in Nonmetropolitan Areas* (Nashville: Abingdon Press, 1967). Judy deals exhaustively on pp. 68-91 with structures of traditional cooperation. A list of contemporary models was made by *Ecumenical Designs: Imperatives for Action in Non-metropolitan America,* prepared by the National Consultation on the Church in Community Life (New York, 1967), pp. 91-93.

compelled to merge with one or more other churches in the years to come.

2) Yoked parish: This type has much in common with the previous type. It differs in the underlying geographical setting. While an extended ministry solves the personnel problems in the collaboration between a town and a country church, the yoked parish consists of two congregations served by one pastor in any geographical proximity, regardless of whether they are urban or rural.[2]

2. MERGER OF CONGREGATIONS. The subject here is variations in the merger of church property.

1) Federated church: This type represents a numerical increase in churches participating in a cooperative model and also indicates changes in the autonomy of the participating congregations. "The federated church consists of two or more congregations of different denominations which unite to form one congregation under Articles of Federation."[3] The participating congregations usually drop their claims to their own church buildings. In that case, one parish provides the ministry for all the other churches, although the others maintain their authority in the administration of matters of their own constituencies. A central worship place for all participating churches is imperative for this model.

2) Union church: This modification of the church merger is a unique phenomenon in the landscape of church cooperation. It shares with the "federated church" the emphasis on the merger of property, yet goes still a step further. A union church comes into existence when several Protestant and non-Protestant denominations share a common ministry, so to speak, under one roof. Only the worship service is held separately. This revolutionary model was tested for the first time in the United States in Kansas City in the fall of 1968 by St. Mark's Church. This church

[2] Judy, *The Cooperative Parish in Nonmetropolitan Areas*, pp. 86-87.

[3] *Ibid.*, p. 87. See Articles of Federation, p. 88.

foundation is the result of ecumenical collaboration between the Catholic Diocese of Kansas City-St. Joseph, the Episcopal Diocese of West Missouri, the Western Association of the Missouri Conference of the United Church of Christ, and the Kansas City Presbytery of the United Presbyterian Church in the USA.

3) Consolidated church: This is the supreme expression of the churchmerger. As one publication puts it, it is "the *organic* union of two or more congregations of two or more denominations. The resultant congregation becomes affiliated with only one denomination." [4] Horace Sills in his book gives several practical examples of church consolidations.[5]

3. PARISH ASSOCIATIONS. Finally, that kind of church type may be presented which proved to be highly successful in the church work of urban congregations. More than type 1 or type 2, this type brings modifications in the degree of cooperation between staff and officers into focus. These parish associations mirror the real experimental character of the entire business of church collaboration. The questions underlying the following discussion are: What are the implications of parish associations for the geographical structure of the resulting formation? What character is assumed by the cooperation of clergy and laymen? How strong is the integration of the analyzed models, i.e., how effective is the unity of the resultant formation despite the autonomy of the participating churches?

1) Enlarged charge: More than any other model, the author believes, this one can become a reasonable remedy for financially trapped congregations. Once two or more congregations of one or more denominations agree on a joint parish program under the direction of one pastor, the enlarged charge comes into existence. The resulting model has to be seen as one unity with several places of worship and congregational gathering. The uniqueness of this model proves to be the participation of lay people. They are the

[4] *Ecumenical Designs,* p. 93.
[5] *Grassroots Ecumenicity,* pp. 11-28.

ones who are in charge of a congregation that cannot afford its own pastor. Accordingly, each church commissions laymen and laywomen who serve on the parish board and in various committees to coordinate the entire parish activity. Since the autonomy of each local congregation is maintained, the lay people take the parish affairs in their own hands, while the minister coordinates the activities between the congregations. The range in cooperation is almost unlimited. Judy gives a number of examples of how this has been done.[6] Surprisingly, the role of the minister in this model brings H. R. Niebuhr's concept of the pastor as "pastoral director" into discussion.[7]

2) Group ministry: More caution should be given to the use of this term. Not every form of parish cooperation is a group ministry. Therefore, more explanation of this point seems imperative. In a group ministry several ministers of two or more independent congregations have agreed on joint action in a given area. This structure is different from the Larger Parish in that each pastor remains in charge of his own congregation. Conversely, it differs also from the Enlarged Charge because of its multiple staff (a team ministry). This model betrays a considerable degree of democratization marked by the formation of *parish councils,* one a lay council, the other a ministerial council. The major part of current inner-city work has assumed the character of the group ministry, of course with variations in the development of administrational procedures. Two outstanding modifications may be identified.

(a) Representational cooperation refers to the fact that the churches, the ministers of which participate in a group ministry, are represented on a "parish council." The *Greater Urban Parish of Minneapolis, Minnesota,* is an example. In 1963 the representatives of five denominations came together in Minneapolis to form the Greater Urban Parish of the Twin Cities. The purpose of this project was stated

<hr />

[6] *The Cooperative Parish,* pp. 77-78.

[7] *The Purpose of the Church and Its Ministry* (New York: Harper, 1956), pp. 90-92.

in these words: "To provide an avenue through which Christian denomination bodies can operate in attracting church and community resources; in strengthening personnel and program in certain selected situations." [8] This group ministry has initiated through a broad variety of programs a number of projects for those people who are trapped by all kinds of needs, especially by poverty and racial disturbance—a day care nursery for preschool children, a twice-a-week tutoring program of junior high students by college students, summer programs for city youth, a psychiatric rehabilitation center, and a music school. How is a group ministry like this organized? Why is it called a "representational" cooperation?

"Representational" means that there are constitutional bodies on the level of the parish operating with democratic procedures. There is an executive and a legislative body. First of all, any of the participating churches may become a sponsor by paying an annual membership fee. The "legislative" body consists of representatives from the congregations. Members elect annually a board of directors. Admitted to the board also are members of organizations in the particular community. The "executive" body is made up of the ministers from the participating congregations. They choose a leader for their team who is an ex officio member of the board; he executes the projects agreed on by the legislative body.

(b) Besides this cooperation called "representational," there is a second one that is brought into operation not by a board and an executive council, but by an individual—in the case following by a minister. He is a kind of coordinator of activities. Because of this "pilot" function (the "steering" function of the minister), this type is called here cybernetic cooperation. *The Methodist Inner City Parish in Atlanta* is an example. In a bulletin issued in March, 1967, when this project was in its fourth year, its goal was defined as follows: "We seek to discover, test and establish new methods of ministry for communities in transition,

[8] *Church in Metropolis* magazine, Winter, 1966, p. 28.

which will be applicable to other cities." As a result, eight Methodist churches work in this cooperative ministry together[9] pursuing the organizational goal. Next, no single congregation offers all services together, but each service is offered by one of the participating churches, each congregation specializing in the service offered. Why is this type termed "cybernetic cooperation"?

It is sufficient to remark here that cybernation refers to an new mode of work. Cybernetics, in its broadest sense, refers to the control or steering process. Applied to church renewal, it means the steering function of an individual in the context of a cooperative ministry. In the case of the Inner City Ministry in Atlanta, this cybernetic function is performed by a clergyman, the "minister to the inner city," who, in 1967, was Dr. Charles E. Wilson, Jr. This cooperative model had a staff in 1967 of three full-time clergymen, eleven seminary interns, two lay workers and approximately thirty-five lay volunteers, all appointed to the cooperative ministry. This ecclesiastical network is kept in operation by the cybernetic function of the inner-city minister, who coordinates the services. It is because of this modification in the coordination of the life of a larger parish that the representational cooperation (through a council) is distinguished from the cybernetic cooperation (through an individual asked to perform the steering function.).

There is hardly any need that cannot be met through one of the helping hands and counseling persons of this cooperative ministry. First of all, there is the young adult center, offering an open house each evening during the week. It serves about two hundred youngsters. Besides the ordinary recreation program, a discussion breakfast is held on Saturday morning for the young adults in the community. Between 9:00 P.M. and 2:00 A.M. the night minister is in charge. Musicians, singers, dancers, bartenders, waiters, hotel clerks, cab drivers, and policemen are his congregation. At Park Street Parish House a pre-school program was

[9] By the end of March, 1967.

121

started to create leadership and thus serve children through Boys' and Girls' Clubs, tutoring programs, study, recreation, and so on. Camp Wesley, located outside Atlanta, serves as a retreat center with all kinds of recreation programs. College-age-men and women are in charge of the supervision. The Trinity Parish House has developed activities involving classes in sewing, ceramics, dancing, and Bible study. Residential ministries is the name of the effort to work together with several churches in the residential area of Atlanta to provide more and better service to the community. The Urban Training Workshop helps to improve the interest in and knowledge of events in the contemporary city life. This is achieved through a nine-hour course over a period of three days. Sociology, psychology, and theology are the fields of study. Welfare Aid is granted in several locations around the city to help people in urgent need.

It is not necessary here to explore further the Methodist Inner City Ministry in Atlanta. In this connection, it suffices to show the "cybernetic" function of a person charged with the coordination of so many services within the cooperative framework of numerous churches. This leads us yet to another type of cooperation.

3) The Larger Parish: Finally, a model can be presented that I am convinced reflects the highest stage in the development of cooperative parish structures. It includes three major elements. The *geographical*: The parish zone of the Larger Parish covers a certain geographical area that is served by the participating churches. The *ecumenical*: Within a geographically limited area, churches agree on close collaboration on the level of structure, organization, and function. The *collegiate*: A new style of ministerial responsibility emerges where the officers in charge of a Large Parish are assigned as staff to the parish rather than to a single local church.

The Larger Parish resembles the group ministry in terms of structure, however with the difference that the multiple staff is, as mentioned before, assigned to the parish as a *whole*. Conversely, it differs from the Enlarged Charge in that the Larger Parish has a *multiple staff* of ministerial leadership serving all participating congregations. In order to come to grips with the complexity of this type, a further distinction may be helpful. Within the Larger Parish type we can identify two subtypes:

(a) The Independent organization is a type of Larger Parish that appears as a structural and organizational organism, the components of which, however, are still somewhat autonomous in terms of jurisdiction and administration, although the general program of the Larger Parish is geared by the parish council. Here, diversity is emphasized over unity, and the independence of the participating churches over the interdependence within the whole parish organism.

In the city of Philadelphia four congregations of the United Church of Christ have been combined to form the *Philadelphia Cooperative Ministry.* Each of these churches, located in neighborhoods of the inner city, has a rich experience of church work in this kind of vicinity. Here the motto of collaboration is, "What churches can do together, they ought not to do alone." Archie Hargraves, who did some research on this Philadelphia model, has made the remark: "The four churches recognizing that each faced a tremendous challenge, decided to pool their resources in order to make the most of the challenge. They said: 'Jointly we can provide continuing and adequate leadership to our congregations, secure necessary financial help when needed. . . .' " [10]

This is how the organizational structure of the Philadelphia Cooperative Ministry looks: (1) A pastor was appointed by the ministers of the participating churches to function as their overall director. (2) All programs are planned by a "cooperative council," to which each congregation sends five representatives. (3) Each of the participating churches retains its autonomy. (4) One director of Christian education works with all four churches.

[10] *Stop Pussyfooting Through a Revolution.* (New York: United Church Board for Homeland Ministries, n.d.), p. 14.

The third point indicates that the independence retained by each of the member churches prevents the establishment of a structure in which the autonomy of the single parish would be absorbed by the desire for constructive unity.

(b) A further modification of parish cooperation is the interdependent organization—a type in which the multitude of partial structures has faded away in favor of organic unity. The following example will show that the autonomy of the participating churches is no longer significant if a parish is founded as a fabric whose parts are totally integrated in its unity. In this case, unity is emphasized over diversity, and the interdependence of the parts over the independence of the participating churches.

East Harlem Protestant Parish in New York is such a model. There is an abundance of literature existing about this model.[11] It has been described, analyzed, criticized, and praised from almost every aspect. Without diminishing the work of any other pastor in the field of experimental ministries over the last twenty years, it may be said objectively that the East Harlem Protestant Parish (EHPP) appears today as the decisive step in the postwar period of church renewal in the United States. And yet, in analyzing this parish few people have given primary attention to the overall picture. Hence, the following account takes this lack into consideration and tries to avoid giving yet another random survey of this New York model.

Despite the fact that EHPP is over twenty years old, it is still flexible and continuously changing. It is changing and moving just like everything in East Harlem. "God is at work 'Turning the Parish upside down' by the things which are always happening" wrote one of the staff mem-

[11] George W. Webber, *The Congregation in Mission* (Nashville: Abingdon Press, 1964). Webber, *God's Colony in Man's World* (Abingdon Press, 1960). Bruce Kenrick, *Come Out of the Wilderness* (New York: Harper, 1962). Grace A. Goodman, *The Church and the Apartmenthouse*, pp. 1-10. *Concept* XI, ed. WCC, Sept. 1966, p. 17. *Cities and Churches*, Robert Lee, ed. (Philadelphia: Westminster Press, 1962).

bers recently.[12] The factor of change was always important in the parish, which started in 1948 with only one woman attending the first worship service in a storefront. In this constant flow of change we ask in what direction the struggle of "God's colony in man's world" is moving.

The specific contribution of EHPP to American church renewal can be evaluated appropriately only by those who know the history of that church. It began as a team ministry composed of three pastors and their wives. This was the size of the "congregation" when it started in 1948. There was no gathered congregation yet. During the next few years, however, it grew to a reasonably large congregation that assembled at several different places. Between 1948 and 1952 the EHPP appeared physically in three storefronts where the entire parish life took place. Moore and Day, in their book *Urban Church Breakthrough,* say that "this choice of locale grew out of observations made by the staff of the EHPP: that (1) the store seemed to be a center of community life in East Harlem; (2) the plateglass windows and street-level door made the store front accessible . . . ; (3) numbers of such locations were available at modest rent. [13]

The next step in the development was taken when in 1952 a Presbyterian church (Church of the Ascension) joined the parish, providing for the first time the facilities of a real church building that could be used by the whole parish. By that time the EHPP had four physical sites—three storefronts and one church building. The only administrative body was a steering committee on which laymen and clergyman served. This committee relieved the former, very unstructured group consisting of the ministers who had taken care of the parish affairs in the first years.

In this early phase, the team ministry was held together by four disciplines:

Devotional: Each minister was expected to give every day

[12] Letty M. Russell in *Union Seminary Quarterly Review,* March, 1966, p. 333.
[13] P. 134.

sufficient time to prayer and Bible reading. In addition, the team would meet every week and celebrate at the end the Lord's Supper. Furthermore, every six months the team would spend three days away from East Harlem for spiritual renewal.

Economic: Any amount of money earned by one of the team ministers went to a common fund. The minister got his salary not according to his qualification, but according to the need of his family.

Vocational: The members of the team ministry were expected to submit once a month some aspects of their work as well as future plans.

Political: The minister also would observe the political events in the Harlem community very carefully and, if necessary, take steps toward involvement.

After a time the structure of EHPP changed again. The storefront churches were abandoned, and a second church joined the parish. Now the units of EHPP were the Church of the Ascension, the Church of the Resurrection, central services (office administration, and community service for legal aid) Mental Health Counseling Program, Metropolitan Action and Interpretation (including a community action stimulator, i.e., a metropolitan missionary whose task was to involve people in the metropolitan area in dialogue), Remedial Reading (library, tutoring, college placement). Moreover, the parish became involved with the work of many other groups, the latest of which is Emmaus House.[14] Each of the listed six units has its own structure, budget, program, and so on. Despite these many functions there is a strong feeling of unity in this parish. The interdependent organization of EHPP is guaranteed by the incorporation of each single working unit into the whole of an ecumenical cooperation.

In what direction is EHPP moving from here? According to information from a staff member[15] the next step will be what is called an "open-ended structure of 'unity in

[14] For the program of this project, see pp. 60-63.
[15] Russell, *Union Seminary Quarterly Review*, p. 334.

diversity.' " It may be said today that the present restructuring of the parish began in the fall of 1965. Generally, the image of the EHPP in the future will be that of a cluster of "ad-hoc groups" that function interdependently and according to the special need at a special time by applying a special method of operation. Already "the Group Ministry has been replaced functionally in terms of service by teams of men and women serving the world together in the various units and groups." [16] Even the original emphasis of EHPP —namely, to serve in a geographically limited area—seems to be undergoing drastic reevaluation. In this respect the most striking novelty appeared when one of the staff members wrote recently in a magazine: "It [the EHPP] must decide whether the way of service in East Harlem calls for more and more diversity and ad hoc groups even to the point of loss of the central Parish structure, or whether it leads to more and more extensive cooperation with other church groups, both Catholic and Protestant, with secular groups and agencies, and possibly the extension of its very small zone." [17]

It may be wise for those clergymen who cling slavishly to the older structure of EHPP for imitation in their own congregation to take into consideration that it has changed itself drastically, since society has undergone transformations. What we see happening in the EHPP in terms of restructuring is typical of what occurs at other places, too. Church renewal moves in the direction of a *de*-institutionalzation and *re*-inforcement of lay power on the broadest level. This phase of transition may be called the period of "open-ended" church structures.

SUMMARY

Three major categories of inter-congregational cooperation can be identified: the extended jurisdiction, the merger of congregations, and parish associations. The latter one

[16] *Ibid.,* p. 337.
[17] *Ibid.*

proved to be most experimental. Within this type we identified the enlarged charge, the group ministry, and the larger parish. We saw that in the *enlarged charge* the minister of a self-supporting church is in charge of one or more smaller congregations that cannot afford their own ministers. The *group ministry*, next, has developed forms of cooperation between officers of churches without affecting the autonomy of the participating congregations. The *larger parish*, finally, is a structure where, in addition to the basic forms of cooperation in the group ministry, several ministers serve a certain geographical area within the frame of a sophisticated organization. The autonomy of the participating units undergoes notable changes.

PART II
TYPES OF
FUNCTIONAL MISSION

7
What Is Functional Mission?

Functional mission does not signify a new era of *parish* work, but rather a new era in the missionary proclamation *outside* the parish. Because of the lack of systematic research in this new field of interest, which might be called "experimental church structures," the subsequent definition has grown out of my personal studies. Hence, functional mission is understood as a kind of activity of the church and its representatives whereby people are addressed in their different vocations and interests *outside* the parish at those places where they live, work, and celebrate. This requires on the part of the church a high degree of flexibility as well as profound knowledge of the specific sociological context of the people it addresses. Functional mission is carried on usually by an individual, sometimes by a team of ministers and laymen.

Perhaps in the future we ought to speak of the "missionary construction of the congregation" [1] and "functional mission" instead of parochial and nonparochial services. For centuries we have thought predominantly in *geographical* terms. The social sciences, however, teach us to think more in *functional* terms in order to recognize the social forms that emerge when people bear the Christian witness. Simultaneously, the two polar concepts in orientation of

[1] This is the translation of the German equivalent *Gemeindeaufbau* or, as it was called earlier in this account, "parish ministry."

131

the congregation come to face each other: the Continental-European (predominantly geographically oriented), and the Anglo-American (more functionally oriented).

As was said before, a sound solution would be to speak of the "construction of the congregation" only, once the congregation is seen as a parochial and collective unit that is preparing itself for mission. Functional mission, on the other hand, is the communication of the Christian message in highly differentiated areas of life, carried on in a specialized and *non*-collective fashion.

One of the implications of a fresh approach to new forms of missionary communication is that the traditional understanding of the role of the minister is called into question. The support by a congregation, the claim to communicate with people in a monologue style (sermon), will be dismissed in favor of a new understanding that is summarized in the phrase "the apostolate of the being here and there." High specialization in this office has become the key proficiency of a person called to bear witness to Christ in a technological society.

Although the factor of sociological differences cannot be discussed here in length, brief attention to this complex phenomenon is indispensable. Our question is, What are the symptoms of a society where a great variety of experiments inside and outside the parish have become imperative?

Talcott Parsons, the Nestor of American sociologists, said in a paper that describes some trends of change in contemporary American society: "The United States, as the most fully developed industrial society in history, has undergone, and is continuing to undergo, a grand scale process of differentiation in the structure of the society itself, and in the culture, which expresses and guides its institutions." [2] This process of differentiation takes place in all sectors of life. There is no area that can be excluded from the challenge of differentiation. This is equally true for the church.

[2] *Structure and Process in Modern Society* (New York: The Free Press, 1964), p. 280.

In the 1860's, a desperate act of rebellion against the forces of a new age shook the Selesian society in East Europe. The late German writer, Gerhard Hauptmann, in his play *The Weavers* has depicted how the poor Selesian weavers, who worked day and night at their looms to make a meager living, one day closed ranks and destroyed several of the new mechanical looms. Instinctively they felt that these new machines, taking work away from their homes, were the vanguard of a dawning age characterized by automation. But these Selesian rebels could not turn back the wheels of history. Today, we are in the midst of a process the labor pains of which were not recognized fully by these East European rebels. Specialization is one of the results of this process that has both emptied and enriched our society. A person who wants to rebel today against specialization is a modern replica of the Selesian weaver. Instead of smashing mechanical looms, this person would turn against the switchboards of our industrial complexes and the laboratories in our universities. But this would be an act as desperate as that of the weavers one hundred years ago. The process of differentiation that began with the separation of the place of living from the place of working has just started and cannot be reversed.

And yet, while specialization has become the domain of education, research, and labor, a great many people today are still reluctant to face the consequences of the process of differentiation for their free time life. However, there are indications that things are changing here, too. More and more persons, for instance, expect a high degree of assimilation on the part of other persons in their relationships. The temporary adjustment of the other person to *my* interest has become the criterion for communication among partners in general. The most likable person, for me, will be the one who shows the greatest willingness to adjust to *my* interest. This has become the criterion for the ability to communicate with one another.

This is, in short, the situation in which the church finds itself today. The society expects from her a similarly high degree of adjustment and assimilation to the different sectors of work, life, and interest of the individual person. Accordingly, the relevance of the gospel is dependent upon the willingness and capability of the church to make the Great Commission relevant in an age of technologically determined specialization.

8
Functional Mission to Residential Structures

GENERAL CHARACTERISTICS

In the years following 1960, a revolution in the style of housing took place in the United States. Everywhere multi-apartment house buildings added an unusual element to the stereotype of single-family housing units. What has been a familiar scene in Europe for several decades all at once began to attract many Americans—the living together collectively in apartment buildings. For the church, too, a new field of mission was opened overnight—the apartment-house ministry. After more than seven years of experimentation three major areas in which mission is carried on may be identified: in public housing projects, in middle-class high-rise apartments, and in luxury apartments. In addition, two basic methods of performing this service have developed: apartment-house ministry performed by a minister who does not live himself in the high-rise building, and formation of an apartment-house congregation by a minister who lives with his people in the building.

Taking together the reports of persons who are in charge of apartment-house ministry, the subsequent characteristics may be stated:

1. People with low incomes have good or even intimate relationships with neighbors on the same floor or in the same housing unit. This provides the apartment-house ministry with the opportunity to set up forms of religious organ-

izations on the basis of these already existing neighborhood ties.

2. Different conditions, however, face the apartment-house ministry in high-rise luxury apartments and in middle-income housing. Mobility and the access to almost unlimited opportunities outside the home are the reasons why persons from these income levels have developed a very peculiar life style for which the church has not yet found appropriate forms of religious organization. Grace Ann Goodman, who has done a great deal of research in this area, has come to the conclusion that

the very mobile, especially the "empty-nest" middle-aged couples who had moved back to the city, showed real resistance to in-apartment programs because their lives were already filled with activities in all parts of the metropolis. They used their apartments largely as retreats. In middle and upper income apartment buildings, the ministers encountered resistance stemming from the fact that people who can afford costly apartments . . . don't want to admit they need anything they can't buy.[1]

What many competent persons in this new missionary assignment say is that the apartment house is hardly any longer the most rewarding place for the church to make contacts with people. The real homes of those people are somewhere in the city. Goodman calls these locations away from home, "psychological neighborhoods." Needless to say after all these remarks, these people do not participate in things happening in the geographical neighborhood of their apartment, either. Along with other community agencies, the church is affected considerably. For example, it was this situation that was experienced by a Presbyterian church located within walking distance of the luxury-class Edgewater Apartments in Lakewood, Ohio. This church reports that although 85 percent of its members live in this part of Cleveland, only one percent have their homes in these high-rise buildings. Surprisingly, however, two large downtown Cleveland churches draw twice as many resi-

[1] "End of the 'Apartment House Ministry,'" *Christian Century*, May 10, 1967, p. 616.

dents from these high-rise apartments as any of the churches in the immediate neighborhood of Edgewater Apartments.[2]

3. These facts about the behavior and attitudes of apartment residents in middle and upper income housing create great doubts about the traditional assumption, according to which the residence shapes a person's life style and the church, therefore, would be successful if it would simply develop new activities adequate to the style of apartment-house living. But this is true only for people living in areas of the city where they cannot escape their environment because of economic and racial reasons. For the ministry in these ghettos, Goodman has the comment: "Flourishing ministries have been carried on in these slum areas for two decades. They are properly termed 'poverty ministries' (not 'apartment ministries'), and their shape is the same, whether the people live in two-story walk-up tenements or 20-story public housing apartments." [3]

Is the apartment-house ministry dead, then? Some answer this question affirmatively, and those doing so may be called competent to make this kind of evaluation. And even those who are convinced that the despisers of the apartment-house ministry are mistaken admit that it takes from two to five years before residents are prone to respond positively to invitations from a minister to set up some kind of religious organization within the walls of a modern apartment-house building.

In order to illustrate what has been said so far theoretically, an example will be given for each of the three socio-economic levels of housing.

PUBLIC HOUSING PROJECTS

East Harlem Protestant Parish in New York has not only pioneered in the postwar search for new models of the congregation, it has also been versatile in the design

[2] Figures from 1966.
[3] *Christian Century*, p. 617.

of specialized ministries. Surprisingly, however, its contribution to the apartment-house ministry is less known than is the structure of the parish.

When the parish was formed in 1948, its ministers made the appalling discovery that only 1.5 percent of the people in the area attended a church. Hence, they started a door-to-door calling in the tenements. Since the parish program was already organized, the callers would tell how the child was doing in class, bring supplementary materials for the parents to use at home, and invite them to mother's club or other church activities. But only a very few of those visited found their way to church. Thus, the success of this door-to-door calling was not the increase in church attendance, but the fact that some tenants gathered to form Bible study groups. Interestingly enough, the lay leaders of the Bible study groups continued with calling, which relieved the ministers considerably.

But then, after about one year, the door-to-door calling discontinued. This marked the formal end of a project that was started as an apartment-house ministry. When this service ceased, fortunately the Bible study groups were efficiently in operation and promised to be a missionary power in the public housing units. A door seal saying in both English and Spanish "Welcome in the name of Christ" identified from then on families belonging to the parish. As one of the staff members commented, "Christ is present not only in the buildings and meeting places of our parish, but also in our homes and the world in which we live." [4]

East Harlem Protestant Parish demonstrates very clearly that a religious organization (i.e., the Bible study groups) can be set up on social neighborhood ties already in existence in lower-income housing. And indeed, these Bible study groups became so important that they turned out to be of an almost integrating power for the entire parish structure. East Harlem Protestant Parish had members in each of the multi-story "high rises." For each one a building

[4] From an official parish bulletin.

138

captain was installed. Later, the lay leaders of the Bible study groups took over this responsibility. These block captains helped to get the material from the parish headquarters quickly distributed even to the remotest family. The staff members used to leave their pamphlets and announcements with each block captain, who put it all under the doors of the tenants.

As far as the Bible study groups are concerned, four functions proved to be important: (1) Providing the frame for free expression of ideas, doubts, and all kinds of concerns on the part of the group participants. (2) Gaining a deeper understanding of the Bible. (3) Preparing the Sunday morning worhip service. Since the study groups met every Wednesday, the topic of the sermon to be given on the following Sunday was discussed well in advance.[5] (4) Serving as a link between the parish and the people in the community.

But is this kind of group life nothing other than turning the church outside in and cutting off parish members from the world and sealing off their worldly existence with a narrow spirit nurtured in the Bible study groups? The East Harlem Protestant Parish was aware of this danger and has avoided becoming a conglomerate of Bible study cliques, each circling selfishly around itself. As a matter of fact, the annual rezoning of the parish tried to combat this predicament. Until 1965 these study groups were organized along *geographical* lines with participants convening at that apartment which was closest to each one's home. The annual rezoning, then, changed the membership composition considerably. Another innovation was the organization along *interest* lines, introduced in 1966. Groups were formed consisting of persons interested in special issues like mental health, psychiatry and religion, community organization, and so forth. The unity of this cell-group structure

---

[5] Cf. *Concept* (a pamphlet published by the World Council of Churches), September, 1966, p. 19, where Pauline Webb describes the relation between these study groups and the Sunday morning sermon.

was demonstrated once a year when the group members all met together at the church.

MIXED HIGH AND LOW INCOME
APARTMENT BUILDINGS

The ministry of *St. Augustine's Episcopal Chapel in Washington, D.C.* is an excellent illustration of a project that started as an *experimental* form of apartment-house ministry and turned out as the formation of a *congregation* with its center in the traditional church building. This project was experimental as long as the sanctuary was not yet built, but became less versatile (which does not mean ineffective) and experimental when the goal, set up by the Episcopal Diocese of Washington, was fulfilled—the formation of a congregation in a mixed high and low income apartment building complex.

In the Southwest area of Washington, D.C., private and public housing units were built in the early sixties side by side. By 1965 approximately 12,000 people had found new homes. In the public housing buildings 98 percent of the residents were black. In the costly private housing units the proportion was far lower, namely 20 percent. For the church a very delicate task arose. How was a ministry to be organized in such a sociologically complex context? The Episcopal Diocese decided it ought to be tried in the form of an apartment-house ministry.

For that purpose the Diocese rented an apartment where a young, single clergyman took up his responsibilities late in 1960. But how to start at a place where no contacts at all had been made by any minister before? Some of the experience he brought into this new assignment helped the Reverend Alfred R. Shands avoid the basic mistake in this kind of environment—the mistake of starting with door-to-door calls and trying to appeal to people as families (since no children were allowed in the costly apartment buildings). Instead, Shands contacted those persons and agencies which were likely to give him specific information about the general behavior and attitudes of the residents.

The key to a successful start in this project was the circumstance that Mr. Shands got some names of persons from agency personnel. Then he began to call those people and say, "I met your friend so-and-so at the party last night, and he gave me your name. I wonder if I could drop in and meet you sometime." He contacted these persons on the basis of his being a neighbor. After these preliminary activities he could dare to take the next step—the most difficult and decisive one—of trying to form a worshiping congregation on the house-church basis. The hazard is that clergymen, although the church has experimented on a broad scale with house churches, cannot predict how apartment dwellers in their desire for privacy and anonymity will respond to this idea.

The first worship service in Shand's apartment attracted thirty people. One week later so many people came that they had to move to a restaurant, which was offered to them by the owner without charge. Here the newly formed congregation had plenty of space for new experiments in liturgy. "We have lost the feeling of celebration, the ecstatic part in life," Mr. Shands commented. And he added, "It is a function of the church to point out to people and identify and celebrate the worship going on in the life in the world. A most obvious way today is in the Freedom Movement." [6] As a result, Shands used to illustrate his sermons with audio-visual resources and new pop music.

But what about the ministry among residents in the nearby *public* housing units? Wasn't Mr. Shand's ministry geared from the very beginning to carry on a total service to both black and white? Actually, this apartment-house ministry was expanded when a new bishop arrived in Washington. Through his initiative a program was inaugurated that helped to establish connections between all people of

[6] Goodman, *New Forms for Ecumenical Cooperation for Mission in Metropolitan Areas,* p. 63.

this new living colony. Especially for the children a fine outdoor festival was held in the various courts, with repetitions in the following years. The establishment of a community organization, house churches (each developed its own style), and an educational program for children finally gave this specialized ministry a broad scale.

To sum up, this model may be regarded as the proof that, despite all critical remarks about the apartment-house ministry, success can be achieved. In the case of the Episcopal Chapel in Washington, the minister in charge had established a group that was self-supporting (paying his salary, and so on) only two years later. Although this group got a worship building, everybody involved recalls the unique history leading to the present organizational structure. It shows that specialized ministries sometimes are transformed into permanent congregations. The question is whether the original zeal of renewal stayed with the group when it became a more institutionalized structure.

LUXURY APARTMENTS

"Thank God for the locked door of the high-rise apartment! It brings us up short, and we must struggle again with our presuppositions of mission. I hope the struggles are fruitful, as they have been on the mission field abroad," says the Reverend A. Benton Randolph, who is in charge of the *Edgewater Apartment Experiment in Cleveland.* And according to *Newsweek,* which carried an article on the apartment-house ministry,[7] the more grandiose the building, the tougher it is to infiltrate. The article brings a quotation from Rabbi Herman E. Schaalmann, who serves apartment dwellers in Chicago. "Our structure—complete with its own grocery and swimming pool—remains virtually impregnable. It's self-contained against the community like a resort hotel." These remarks reflect some of the problems a minister has to face who tries to perform a specialized ministry in these expensive and extravagant living boxes.

[7] September 7, 1964.

Against this background the Presbyterian Church in the USA began in 1964 an experiment that concluded in 1966. Mr. Randolph had a very laborious start in this special assignment. Before he could begin contacting residents, he launched some preparatory work, without which no apartment-house ministry is any longer possible. First, he managed to mail three sets of explanatory papers about his expectations to local clergy, apartment residents, and apartment owners. Then he contacted the clergy from the churches in the immediate vicinity and asked for names of their parishioners living in Edgewater Towers. The next step was to check with the management, since it did not permit door-knocking in any form. Again, here as well as in the Washington project, the beginning is the most delicate part of the whole undertaking and requires sensitivity and sociological training on the part of the minister.

Having the names of 150 Protestant residents, Mr. Randolph finally started contacting these persons by telephone. He tried to make appointments. By that time, he intended to organize his ministry into three sections: (1) In the apartments, (2) Outside the apartments, in meetings with clergymen from nearby churches. Randolph used to hold luncheon discussion groups with those ministers or accepted speaking engagements. (3) In the management. He served as an observer at a trainee program of an apartment firm, also as an adviser for the disign of new apartments.

When he talked personally to the residents for the first time, Randolph never mentioned religion. He chatted on a very general level. From each visit he made a record, although he never took notes during the conversation. Seventy percent of those he talked to did not mention religion at all while discussing their life style and interests. When it came to the formation of small study groups, the limitations of the apartment-house ministry became very obvious. Since he could not make contacts with those persons who were not members of the nearby churches, his service was geared almost exclusively to work with church members. Randolph in Cleveland had the same experience as did his colleague in Lincoln Towers in New York—the gathering of fellow tenants for a study or worship group does not work out.

The further development of the Cleveland project can be described briefly. Since activity was restricted to church members who happened to live in the apartment buildings, several forms of religious organizations were tried. There was a group dealing with interpersonal relations, for instance. In this activity, it was found that the ideal size for such a group is fourteen. Later, more solid relations to the management firm were established. Yet, despite all these activities, the question remains, Has the apartment-house ministry a future? Critics say no. And, indeed, some experiences seem to confirm this dim outlook.

9
Functional Mission to Vocational Structures

The French worker-priest Henri Perrin, who was killed in 1954 under mysterious circumstances, wrote shortly after the Second World War a letter in which he raised the question:

Why has the social force of the church faded into nothingness? Because it has not penetrated the world of the worker. Factories with 9,000 men have a dozen-odd Christian trade unionists. . . . The union leaders are involved in the factory and the priest is removed from it; he could only get in if he became a worker. No priest has dared to re-establish the primitive law of Christianity and go to work alongside those he wants to convince.[1]

Since the time Perrin wrote that letter, we have made only small progress in the solution of this predicament. Yet, isn't there something like a functional mission to vocational structures? Let us see whether there are new answers to an old problem.

Indeed, there is something like industrial mission. Compared with the initial stages, it has undergone a remarkable refinement. Industrial mission, as soon as it found a starting point *outside* the industrial plant, became a functional mission to vocational structures in general. The industrial mission, which originated in England,[2] today has become a specialty of functional mission in the United States. In 1950

[1] *Priest and Worker: The Autobiography of Henri Perrin* (New York: Holt, Rinehart & Winston, 1964), p. 89.
[2] *Presbyterian Life* magazine, October 1, 1966, p. 6; and November 1, 1966, p. 19.

the Institute for Industrial Relations was founded in Chicago. Six years later the Detroit Industrial Mission began to operate, the first organized project on American soil. Today twelve projects are bound together in the National Committee for Industrial Mission.[3] Three others are in the process of construction.

Five areas of industrial mission may be identified: (1) financial institutes, (2) research laboratories, (3) commercial sectors, (4) urban and state institutions, and (5) industry. We will deal here with the first four, leaving out the fifth type, since industrial mission performed, for instance by Detroit Industrial Mission, is largely known.[4] Instead we will concentrate on those which still need to be introduced to a wider public. In order to reorganize the material, three working styles are differentiated and related to experiments: (1) the dialogue-conference type, (2) the action-reflection type, and (3) the communication-consultation type.

THE DIALOGUE-CONFERENCE TYPE

Those industrial missions which make extensive use of dialogue with people at the particular places of work or of the wide variety of conference styles are called here dialogue-conference type. Dialogue and conference enlarge the functional mission to vocational structures through a counseling and issue-shaped (competence in the field) program. Accordingly, the *dynamics* of functional mission in this area are dependent upon the development of a new style of communication; the *connotation* of the message, on the other hand, relies on the capabilities of the person in charge to uncover the significance of the particular job situation in the light of the Christian faith.

1. FINANCE: WALL STREET MINISTRY IN NEW YORK. Over 400,000 people commute daily to downtown Manhattan.

[3] Founded in 1966.
[4] Scott I. Paradise: *Detroit Industrial Mission, a Personal Narrative* (New York: Harper, 1968).

The majority are employed in or around Wall Street. Forty-one percent of them spend two hours on their way to and from their working places. This is a classic illustration of the separation of working and living place. Anyone who has ever walked through the Wall Street area and realized that a major part of the world's money is managed there cannot help raising the question of what methods of operation are needed for a ministry that proclaims the ultimate concern not in terms of dollar-power but in terms of faith-power.

The Wall Street Ministry calls itself "experimental, industry centered, ecumenical, and non-parochial." Four presuppositions guide its operation:

1. The separation of the place of residence from the place of work has a parallel in the gap between what the local church proclaims to the people on Sunday and what the church members experience during the week in the context of their work. The formation of the Wall Street Ministry in 1966 is a partial answer to this challenge caused by compartmentalization.

2. The structure and policy of modern financial institutions make an examination of theological presuppositions imperative. Since the tradition of Christian thought is so pluralistic, the Wall Street Ministry puts overt emphasis on certain doctrines of the church, neglecting others; yet it does not sell out the depth of the Christian faith. A pamphlet says, referring to the spiritual needs arising in the world of the finance employee, ". . . his [the minister's] theology may not speak to the person whose main experience in life is not one of suffering, but one of success, where main need is not to know of God of the Cross so much as to know the God of creativity and initiative." Hence, more emphasis on a theology of power characterizes the theological basis of proclamation in the Wall Street area.

3. Before the Wall Street Ministry could dare to go into operation, the church's own relationship to the economic order had to be examined.

4. Another extremely important question that had to be answered before this project could start was, What does the life style of people who are employed in the area of finance look like? Research made by the Wall Street Ministry confirmed what the Detroit Industrial Mission found out long before, that man in our industrial society is oriented toward (1) reliance upon science and technology, (2) rationalized organization, and (3) the pragmatic spirit.

After two years of preparatory studies, the Wall Street Ministry began in 1967, first with official contacts in the Wall Street district. This ministry is organized as a "non-profit membership corporation." Its function is performed by a board of trustees and a staff consisting of a full-time clergyman, a part-time secretary, and a part-time seminarian assistant. Twenty-one trustees represent six Christian denominations and the Jewish community. Fourteen are laymen who have their offices in downtown Manhattan. The Wall Street Ministry is financed by the Episcopal Church, the United Church of Christ, and the United Presbyterian Church.[5]

On the sixteenth floor at 55 Liberty Street in New York, the visitor finds a door with a sign "Wall Street Ministry." Here the Reverend Francis C. Huntington, director of the project, has a three-room office. The methods of operation the Wall Street Ministry is pursuing are as secular as those of other corporations that share office space on the same floor. As mentioned, the dominating working style is conferences and issue-shaped conversations between the executives of the Wall Street Ministry and representatives from business and finance.

One of the typical invitations sent out to the financial community reads, "Value Systems and the Individual: What Are the Bases for Ethics in Today's World? Alternate Thursdays, November 2 through December 14; 12:15–1:30 P.M." Then follows a brief description of the seminar

[5] The Catholic Church participates in the project through the Paulist Fathers.

148

curriculum. Those who are interested gather at that time in Mr. Huntington's office for a luncheon sponsored by the Wall Street Ministry. According to an official report, there were five different luncheon seminars (each meeting four or six times) and more than twelve additional meetings during the first year of operation. Over fifty persons at the executive level in a variety of occupations participated. How are the conferences conducted? Three forms have developed so far:

1) The "Case Material" Conference. With case studies at hand, one particular seminar tried to examine the sources of authority on which people rely in their daily decision-making. One of the practical cases discussed was the problem of what the partners of a small brokerage firm should do with a presently ineffective employee who has been with the firm twenty-five years and has only eight years to go before retirement. Mr. Huntington frequently uses material produced by the Detroit Industrial Mission. In addition to these seminars, where case studies are presented to the group or even produced by participants, Huntington[6] interviewed some fifty-five salesmen in ten different firms, the results of which provided the Wall Street Ministry with new themes for conferences.

2) The Special Issue Meeting. In June of 1967, the Wall Street Ministry called for a luncheon meeting at the New York Chamber of Commerce to hear a report on the controversial role the church played during the Eastman Kodak dispute. This sort of conference shows the intention of the Wall Street Ministry to present current issues of social-ethical importance as soon as possible to the business community.

3) The Academic Conference. This type of conference involves students, professors, and research personnel. On one special occasion the Wall Street Ministry together with a large metropolitan church sponsored a two-day conference for business school students in business ethics. Ac-

[6] He himself once took fourteen weeks of registered representative training with a major brokerage house.

cording to a report issued by Mr. Huntington's office, "the participants were very enthusiastic and welcomed the chance for some cross-fertilization of theological, sociological, economic, and practical business points of view." On another occasion the Wall Street Ministry conducted an evening seminar for five theology students who held summer jobs in business.

Here is not the place to evaluate this type of functional mission. But it may be stated that Mr. Huntington and his staff (a second minister is intimated) have established for the first time communication between the church and the world of finance in the framework of a specialized ministry. This $44,000 project (in 1967) has involved businessmen through person-to-person dialogue and conferences in a creative exchange of concerns. The Wall Street Ministry has linked together two realms that allegedly had nothing to do with each other.

2. RESEARCH LABORATORIES. *Boston Industrial Mission* (BIM), incorporated in 1964, is the first to concentrate on the area of research and development. And indeed, the challenge to the church in the Boston area is tremendous. In and around Boston lie more than two hundred corporations engaged in research and development. Thousands of qualified engineers and research persons are engaged in the devolopment of electronics and computer systems. In this part of New England, the Second Industrial Revolution is in progress. For this purpose, hundreds of Ph.D.'s are produced at nearby Harvard University and the Massachusetts Institute of Technology. Because of this high potential in research and leadership a new approach to industrial mission became imperative, if the church was not to lose the scientific leadership of the future.

Scott I. Paradise, at present executive director of BIM, had worked with the Detroit Industrial Mission before he came to Boston. According to an observation he made during the last two years, three kinds of people should be identified in the area of the research and development industry.

"The *business*-oriented lived in a world of sales, profits, investments, growth and sometimes fierce competition. The *managers* wrestled with production schedules, personnel problems, and costs. And the *engineers and scientists* had their own distinct interests, problems." And he adds, "Among these men I found to my surprise that their work, though fun and interesting, was often felt to be unsatisfactory because they felt it lacked direct bearing on our most urgent social crisis." How is a functional mission to deal with this problem adequately?

First of all, the structure of BIM is very similar to the Wall Street Ministry. There is a board of trustees, consisting of research personnel, sociologists, theology professors, and pastors, the executive director himself, and his associate. Since BIM is a conference and dialogue type, its work is based on a "getting acquainted, seeking encounter" technique combined with a "working group" (called experimental groups) and "seminar-style" concept. In short, the missionary serves as a counselor and study group enabler in the specific context of the research industry. His task is to practice the "apostolate of the being here" in a very sophisticated segment of our technological society.

What can a minister do once he is assigned to functional mission in such an area and arrives at the place of his future activity without knowing anybody? This is the general problem of each functional mission. Accordingly, the function of the minister will be twofold: (1) to make initial contacts on a very informal basis, and (2) to deepen contacts through the application of more formal devices. In the case of BIM these are:

1) Meetings with individuals in the context of their work in their offices, laboratories, and cafeterias. Mr. Paradise started his activity by calling several persons whose names he had obtained earlier. Through these cautious initial contacts he obtained the addresses of other persons. Luncheon meetings with them gave him the opportunity to learn about their problems and expectations of the church.

2) Attending meetings of professional groups of engineers and scientists.

3) Convening and participating in informal discussion groups set up to explore the human and social implications of industrial life and work. These "experimental groups" have focused on different subjects. Business ethics proved to be a very popular item. As a result of setting up these groups, either the missionary's suggestion or those of other interested persons were followed in arranging schedules and outlines. One Catholic layman, for instance, convened a group of persons from business and management for a discussion on current ethical conflicts.

Besides organizing other study groups, Mr. Paradise held luncheons with engineers and scientists in the office of a company. This group met for eighteen months. The issue most worthy of study, it seemed for this group, was the impact of certain technical inventions on ethical decision-making in economy and politics.

4) Studying and writing about the issues, and recording and evaluating the experiences. The minister in the position of functional mission assumes the role of a reporter who informs his denomination about success and failure in his ministry. After the first two years of experimentation, Mr. Paradise wrote in a report: "From my point of view, our theology as we have received it, proved in these discussions to be entirely inadequate to come to grips with the life and work in a scientific establishment." [7] At this point the importance of the feedback function becomes apparent. The teaching function of the church is challenged by the demand to examine its theological presuppositions.

3. COMMERCIAL: THE AGORA SHOPPING CENTER MINISTRY IN OAKBROOK, ILLINOIS. During the past decade shopping has become a national habit. Shopping centers are something like local Meccas for modern consumers. Pop's grocery store at the corner is almost dead today, and the spacious exhibition halls of ambitious firms have a profitable

[7] From a bulletin of BIM.

future. Shopping centers are the fortresses of white capitalism in the suburbs. Some clergymen have already recognized the new challenge and have felt a call for a new style of ministry. One of these new projects is the Agora Shopping Center Ministry in Oakbrook, Illinois.

The merchandising community of Oakbrook in suburban Chicago has over fifty stores and employs approximately three thousand people. This is the population of a small town. As anybody knows, where this many people live and work together, tensions and problems arise. This is what draws members of the merchandising community in growing numbers to the Reverend Donald N. Kelly for assistance. "Our employees aren't getting along with us or with each other. I feel we've lost communication," an executive from a nearby department store told Mr. Kelly one morning. His client presented a very typical case that makes the presence of the church at a place like this imperative. "A good share of my counseling," Kelly says, "goes on at coffee breaks or lunch time. I find the informal atmosphere can be a definite asset. Agora's ultimate aim must be to influence the business structure itself." [8]

Basically, the church can assume two major forms of structure in this environment of the shopping center. One possibility is to relocate a congregation that already existed at another place in the shopping center and make her adjust to the new setting as a full replacement of the lost sanctuary. This is the case, for instance, in Philadelphia where the Church on the Mall [9] came into existence as the result of the change in the social milieu. This type of congregation was characterized as a "shopping center church."

Yet, a further possibility is the development of functional mission to the shopping center community. This means to start right from the spot *without* the support of a congregation. The goal of such a ministry is to minister to the needs of the merchandising community without the intention of forming a religious organization in the shopping

[8] From *The Kiwanis* magazine, February, 1966.
[9] See pp. 52-53.

center. Functional mission in the shopping center means to unwrap the church like an article in order to bring her back to the marketplace. Says Truman Douglass, executive vice-president of the United Church Board of Homeland Ministries, which has sponsored the Agora Ministry in Oakbrook, "She (the church) must meet people where they carry on their most vital tasks." Already during the development of the shopping center area, the United Church of Christ leased a 600-square-foot space in one of America's largest and busiest shopping centers. In 1964, finally, Mr. Kelly undertook in a modern office the functional mission to the Oakbrook community.

Accordingly, the structure of this specialized ministry is again dialogue-conference oriented. Mr. Kelly is a counselor ("a ministry of listening"), an enabler of ad hoc seminars, and a consultant to the business community. If this may be termed the outer structure of this ministry, the inner structure of this unique adventure in functional mission is marked by the specific problems arising in the merchandizing community—tensions in the management and among employees, the ethical implications of business policy, the job frustrations of the individual, the complicated decision-making process of firms, and so on.

Mr. Kelly spends most of his time counseling or being consulted. Says one salesman, "It's a relief to stop in at Don's, have a coffeebreak, and talk and patch up the problem, which might otherwise grow in size." Thus, the basic method of this part of Kelly's assignment is the application of counseling and psychotherapeutic measures. A minister in this position must have an excellent command of counseling practice. This, indeed, was one of the prerequisites for getting the job. This informal counseling is one activity. Many times, however, people from the firms or department stores make appointments for counseling that may last over a longer period. One morning, for example, three executives came to see Kelly. The first was not sure if he had done the right thing when he fired an employee for stealing. That fellow worked for the company for twenty years. The second client discussed with Kelly the problem of understanding between the employees and the management. The third presented a problem that revealed enough difficulties to enter into long-term counseling. He simply was at the end of his rope, because he could not find satisfaction any longer in his work.

Later that morning Kelly met with some salesgirls at their coffeebreak. They had run into problems with the new quota systems. Yet, how shall a minister deal with such a problem if he does not know from practical experience the psychological stresses emerging in this situation? Kelly decided to work that afternoon as a salesman at one of the big department stores. This kind of flexibility always accompanies functional mission like this one. As Kelly understands it, the merchandizing community is the area of responsible action.

So much for the dialogue function of the Agora ministry. What about the conference style? Similar to luncheon seminars held by the Wall Street Ministry in New York, Agora conducted a novel-reading group between noon and 1:00 P.M. Quite a number of participants came to appreciate discussion opportunities on human depth problems during the lunch hour. Another approach at involving the merchandizing community was the Art Festival. For this program invitations were sent out to business people and artists alike. Agora was open for coffee and refreshments from 9:00 A.M. through 6:00 P.M. during both days of the fair. Approximately a dozen paintings and pieces of sculpture borrowed from a collection were on display. In addition the film "The Parable" was shown. The discussion afterwards was lively because of the presence of five artists and their spouses.

But Agora—since it is an experimental ministry—had not yet found its final shape. The trend goes in the direction of more involvement of lay people who could conduct seminars. But a beginning has been made. Said one member of the Oakbrook community recently, "Oakbrook is a much better place since the coming of Agora."

THE ACTION-REFLECTION TYPE

The ministry to vocational structures is so manifold that a further differentiation is necessary. So far we have dealt only with what was called the dialogue and conference type. One of the most pioneering adventures in functional mission, however, would not fit this description. Thus the introduction of another type becomes necessary. This is the *action-research* method of performing functional mission. According to this philosophy, mission in the urban context is seen as a research activity combined with reflection about the findings and results. The action-research type emphasizes that research of urban institutions has developed a new kind of mission. The missionary is involved in contacts with people at their working places as well as in reflection about what he has performed. The latter activity takes place in cooperation with his colleagues. A good illustration is a project formed in Philadelphia.

High above the busy streets of downtown Philadelphia a minister sits in his modern office directing a unique adventure in functional urban mission. It is the Reverend Jitsuo Morikawa, executive director of the *Metropolitan Associates of Philadelphia* (MAP). This minister is guided by a philosophy that is briefly this: "To obey the Lord, to keep pace with his activities of renewal and change, is to live in constant experimentation grounded in the discipline of action-research. But research can no longer be what it has been, a highly specialized activity of the church, but must become normative in church life."[10] Why is MAP unique?

In recent years theologians have come to recognize that functional mission becomes narrow if it addresses persons, *individuals,* only. What about the collectivity, the institutions? At this point MAP comes in. Morikawa and his staff believe that a ministry to *institutions,* especially in the urban setting, has become imperative. Hence, MAP has to be seen as functional mission to man in the context

[10] Jitsuo Morikawa, "The Calling of the Nations," *Church in Metropolis* magazine, Fall, 1966, p. 19.

of urban institutions by which he is guided more or less consciously in his everyday life.

MAP was formed in 1965. More than sixty clergymen and lay people work together in a team that is likely to set new accents for future mission in the American city. Morikawa and his friends have emphasized from the very beginning that the uniqueness of MAP lies in the combination of social research and theological reflection about what staff members have learned while working in urban structures. "Action-research is a celebrative act," Morikawa believes. "It is the church engaged in the exciting enterprise of discerning where and how God is at work renewing his world in order to respond and participate with him. This is the church's worship and obedience in celebrative thanksgiving, so that the task of action-research is not a burden to endure, but a joyful search for signs of the kingdom." [11]

The Associates distinguish themselves at three points from previous examples of functional mission to vocational structures: (1) They work in *secular jobs*. (2) The strategy of missionary action aims at *urban institutions*. (3) The missionary function is not primarily proclamation, but serves as research for the *presupposition of secular mission*.

A further analysis of MAP shows that it has applied three major elements of current church renewal to its work: (1) The idea of the working and simultaneously "missionarizing" minister (priest). This is the underlying basis of the French worker-priest concept. (2) The idea of the total emancipation of the laity, i.e., the realization of the thesis that a theologically trained layman can more than just replace a worldly oriented theologian. (3) The idea of the secular city as the prime field of missionary activity. This makes sense in a time when commercial skyscrapers have replaced medieval cathedrals.

As mentioned, the combination of research and theological reflection plays an overt role in MAP. This means noth-

[11] *Ibid.*

ing less than reconciling sociology and theology on the field of mission. Both disciplines, MAP believes, can be worked out simultaneously. Hence, an "action-theology" triology shall help to realize that: (1) the *theology* of social change passes on the knowledge of how previous generations evaluated God's acting in history. (2) The *sociology* of social change explores the dynamics of relationships between the individual and groups, of the social roles of the individual in the urban context. (3) The *service* of social change is the giving away of people to one another by great deeds of love. The question arises, How do the Associates realize this philosophy?

Each new approach to mission creates a new style for those involved. "The concern is to bring together a microcosm of the city itself in cross-disciplinary reflection and research." Hence, three different groups of staff personnel have developed:

1) The worker ministers: Clergymen who have taken secular positions in various structures of the city—for instance, poverty planning, real estate selling, or urban redevelopment.

2) The urban agents: Theologically trained persons, mostly clergymen, who are involved in significant events occurring in the life of Philadelphia. Their function is to investigate and report about the development in three concerns of the city: politics and government, education and the arts, business and industry.

3) Lay associates: Laymen from the Philadelphia area who show concern for a deeper understanding of human life conditions in the context of a certain profession. These persons devote extra time after their daily work to reflect and share with other groups experiences in their profession.

From his fourth-floor office on South Thirteenth Street director Morikawa co-ordinates MAP, of which lay associate and Harvard law graduate Gregory Harvey says it has "more of a practical application of Christian theology to the problems of the city than in any other group I've known." MAP is like a spider's web laid upon the structure of the city, which is divided into six activities: politics, industry and economics, welfare, art and education, organization, zoning and ecology. In each of these divisions works a group composed of a cross section from the three basic staff groups listed above. After their work MAP volunteers, who spend about an extra five hours each with this activity a week, meet in a so-called sector conference. In these sessions they hear reports from colleagues and discuss their concept of Christian existence in a secular context. Because of this emphasis on reflection, the whole project was characterized here as the "action-reflection" type.

What is this new adventure in functional mission, which costs $116,000 annually, for? The most important function, besides productive reflection and a "hidden" missionary effort, lies in the feedback function of MAP to the contributing denominations and agencies—American Baptists, Episcopalians, Lutherans, the United Church of Christ, and the National Council of Churches. Besides, many local churches in the Philadelphia region have come to know over the last three years that Morikawa's dim outlook on the layman's role proved to be premature, at least for MAP. Morikawa had said, "The church today is immersed in talk about mission. But little is being done to test out how the laity can participate in missionary action in the public institutions of modern metropolis." [12]

COMMUNICATION-CONSULTATION TYPE

The third type of functional mission to vocational structures is an even less "direct" mission than the ones previously mentioned. The characteristic of the communication-consultation type is that it represents "mediating" mission, i.e., the church assigns its missionaries to activities in a certain vocation in order to collect knowledge about the relation of work and religion at places where people work. The prime responsibility of such mediating mission is that the missionary starts listening *before* he begins to organize

[12] *United Church Herald* magazine, September, 1967, p. 9.

his activities. "Mission" in this type is, first of all, the living and thinking together of missionary and worker. The communication of mission, so to speak, occurs through the channel of mediation. As a result, the missionary after a certain time appears to be trustworthy and becomes a consultant. This peculiar communication-consultation type has grown out of the church's recognition that mission is relevant today only if a careful preparatory work has been achieved. This concept of mediating mission is certainly a great step toward a new understanding of the function of the church in the area of vocation.

An example is *Ecumenical Associates in Lansing, Michigan*. Actually, the title "Ecumenical Associates" is not a very imaginative name for a ministry to the state government of Michigan, which is located in Lansing. Ecumenical Associates is a three-year cooperative project supported by four denominations. It started in 1967 when two ministers, the Reverend Charles W. Millar and the Reverend Robert H. Richardson, came to Lansing in order to tie connections with representatives from executive and legislative branches of government. They hoped to deepen the mutual understanding of political and ethical tasks in current society. On the other hand, the Associates assumed the obligation to report to their denominations about their experiences in ministry to governmental institutions. This feedback function enables the church to deal more effectively with issues related to the realm of government. Regarding this feedback function, it is said in a pamphlet, "Its purpose is to develop a staff and specialized program to help clergy and laypeople exercise their traditional citizenship responsibilities in public affairs more thoughtfully, articulately, and effectively."

This team ministry has strict orders to remain neutral in its contacts with governmental officials. "Ecumenical Associates by the terms of its incorporation and its clearance from the Internal Revenue Service," as a position paper says "is strictly limited to educational and charitable purposes. The staff is prohibited from taking positions in respect to partisan public issues, and it may not attempt in any way to influence legislation." The question arises of how an effective ministry is possible under these circumstances.

Before an answer is tried, a further explanation of the structure is needed. The entire project was developed as a three-year program. The particular goals of each year set the criteria for the methods of mission. The first year, starting with 1967, focused on the development of staff experience in public affairs. The second year, 1968, saw the staff enabling discussion groups with persons active in public affairs and trying to explore the ethical dimensions of their work. Also in the second year, the staff began feedback activities to their denominations. The third year will expand the work—in what direction the subsequent account tries to show.

First year: In this initial phase of their functional mission, the two ministers participated in a variety of internships.

1) In the executive branch of the government, Governor Romney gave permission for a three-month internship in his office.

2) In the legislative branch an internship of the same length of time was granted for the other minister.

3) In order to make contacts with responsible persons in other parts of the executive branch, the ministers called on several administrative departments in state government.

4) Since the understanding of governmental work today is only partial and incomplete without a knowledge of the role pressure and interest groups play, the staff entered into the study of lobbyism.

5) For a deepening of their personal knowledge in this field the staff was also encouraged to take courses in political science at the University of Michigan or Michigan State University.

Second Year: As the project moved into its second year, this present book was underway. Hence, I shall mention the projections worked out in advance. Besides the deepening of relations to representatives from executive and legislative branches, the beginning of educational programs was being considered. This stage of functional mission to the state government saw the staff discussing with denominational executives the relationships of church people to public affairs. According to the position paper, the issues were to be "the clarification of the theological and political issues which are raised where churches and church people show interest in public affairs. The purpose of these discussions will be to lay the ground work for developing discussions and study materials to be used with clergy and laity." [13] Ecumenical Associates was to add a third person to the staff during its second year of operation. The overall responsibility of the staff would be to convene groups, stimulate discussions, and write outlines for use with similar groups.

Third Year: As planned, this stage was to take place in 1969. The major obligation for the three ministers was to continue work on the development of study material and to make a general summary in the form of various recommendations to the denominations:

1) The development of further study material for church people.

2) Short-term internship programs in public affairs for clergy and lay people.

3) Involvement of seminary students in the work of the Associates. Those seminarians are expected to participate through internships. As the position paper points out, it was suggested by the late Robert Spike of the University of Chicago that such an internship would meet the needs of some students in the fourth year of a new doctoral program at the University of Chicago designed to prepare men for specialized ministries in the churches.

This is, in short, a report on what has been accomplished so far. After the completion of this project in December, 1969, a critical evaluation will decide if this type of func-

[13] From the pamphlet *Ecumenical Associates: A Summary of the Project.*

tional mission can be recommended to the churches as a permanent structure of missionary involvement in the area of vocation. The Center for the Scientific Study of Religion at the University of Chicago is most likely to serve as an evaluation committee.

10
Functional Mission to Poverty Structures

Outdating the old-fashioned methods of being charitable, a new challenge urges the church to deal with poverty in an unprecedented way. Poverty in earlier times was the great summoning for the church in terms of expressing the virtues of mercy and charity. In our time, however, a functional mission to poverty in a very different way has become imperative because it proves to be a power, a structure, which demands a highly sophisticated approach on the part of the church if anything important is to be done. To get involved in the war on poverty requires knowledge of the dynamics in this area. Some churches have not stayed outside. Out of their participation they created specific forms of functional mission to poverty structures.

CHRISTIAN SOCIAL SERVICE CENTER

The two examples described below differ basically from what was called earlier in this book "communal participation."[1] Certainly, functional mission to poverty structures includes forms of communal participation, too. But what is the communal participation for? Actually, communal participation is a *method* only, but functional mission to poverty structures is the *content* of an action. The content consists of very specific programs for poverty stricken areas and their

[1] See p. 106.

people in need. The first one is what may be called the Christian Social Service Center.

A good example is the *Broadway Christian Center in Indianapolis, Indiana*. In the inner city area of Indianapolis, at Broadway and Seventeenth Street, a considerable change in the social composition of the population took place during the early sixties. Surrounded by a growing number of Negro families, Third Christian Church steadily lost ground among the diminishing white constituency in the neighborhood. Finally in 1963 the church board decided to relocate the church. Again a church board had lost its social conscience. The Sirens of suburban church life had deafened the ears of both laymen and minister. As a result, Third Christian Church left an old brick building with adequate facilities behind. Some denominational executives and concerned ministers immediately recognized the change that arose then. There was an abandoned church building in a low-income area with people living in deteriorated homes with no hopes whatsoever (the median length of school attendance was 10.2 years in 1960). Finally, money was raised and an experimental project started that bore the name Broadway Christian Center. It opened its doors in 1963.

Run by a staff of two in 1968—a minister-director and an associate, who happens to be Negro—this project serves as a center for dozens of programs for people in need. In the first place, it serves the social and spiritual needs of approximately 40,000 people living in the area of the abandoned parish. The second objective is the establishment of a self-supporting congregation. In its third and final phase, the center hopes to become a training institute of religious leadership for the inner city. But still it struggles through its first phase trying to develop a new style of functional mission to poverty structures.

To say "poverty structures" instead of just "poverty" is reasonable today, since poverty appears as a labyrinth of human need, as a system of desperation and hopelessness. This is exactly the background of the center in Indianapolis.

For the staff it became crystal clear from the very beginning that an effective functional mission to poverty structures today requires a multi-structured, inventive, and flexible program. Accordingly the center, a $62,000-a-year project, has "specialized" for the time being in the formation of a very broad program with possibilities for helping in manifold situations of need.

Because of its function of being a place of permanent availability, Broadway Christian Center has indeed met many needs. It has done so on three major levels:

1) Provision of space in its building for many agencies and groups that serve or are expected to serve the neighborhood. The only requirement for using the building is that the offered service or activity be performed on an interracial and intercultural basis. For instance, the center opened its doors to two congregations that were looking for space to meet. Furthermore, for more than three years a public school branch used several rooms. The list of those agencies connected with the work of the center is large. It includes the Education Committee of the Mayor's Commission on Human Rights, the Public Health Service, the Planned Parenthood Incorporation (for postnatal counseling), and several welfare agencies. In addition, legal service is offered for those who are on trial. Needless to say, political meetings take place, too, at the center.

2) Besides having many agencies come and use the facilities, the center has contacts with other institutions on the basis of joint action. Thus, it functions as a mediator between public offices (of private agencies) and the people from the neighborhood. Relationships were started with a Black Power Community Center. Staff persons hold membership in the Indiana Council of Churches, the Board of Public Safety, and the Housing Cooperation of the Church Federation. Recently, the center applied for affiliation with the Community Service Council of Metropolitan Indianapolis.

3) As the basis for the cooperative network held together through the Broadway Christian Center, activity in com-

munity organization appears to be most likely. This non-professional community organization includes home visitations, conferences with individuals and groups, employment solicitation and referral, housing investigation, and provision of direct aid through food and clothing allotments. The center is also organizing block clubs. By 1967, there were eight clubs; there were two when the project started. The goal is to make these block clubs independent, self-operating, and self-supporting associations with a genuine leadership. Finally, Broadway Christian Center sponsors an expansive recreation program for the neighborhood youth. There is plenty of space to do that. Right across the street is a playground. In addition, summer school was held with forty-five pupils enrolled. It included activities like picnics, play, and visits to the post office and library. Intern students usually served as instructors.

Broadway Christian Center has, as this analysis tries to show, developed a broad variety of services responding to the broad scale of needs in the community. Here we see the modern style of a functional mission to poverty structures as performed by a Christian social service center. The other efficient means is the involvement of the church in a community organization.

INVOLVEMENT IN COMMUNITY ORGANIZATION

A second major method of performing functional mission to poverty structures is the involvement in community organization. But this is not the proper place to describe in length methods of a community organization. What shall be done, instead, is to show what the role of the church in a community organization program is. Two ways of getting involved may be identified: (1) through nonprofessional community organization, and (2) through professional community organization.

A good example of the first type is the *Lake County Inner City Task Force in Gary, Indiana*. Surprisingly, this city with considerable social tension was spared from riots during the hot summer of 1967, when Detroit and

Newark exploded. After that summer went by without major troubles in Gary, a group of ministers and laymen, which was organized as the Inner City Task Force, decided to use the time of respite, which a favorable destiny had granted to the city of Gary, to deal effectively with the problems of the troubled community. The question they raised was, How can the religious community provide leadership, not just in preventing riots or keeping the lid on, but in dealing with the "troubling ferment of social change"? As a result of these consultations, a meeting of ministers and laymen was called in September, 1967, to form a planning committee that was expected to begin a community organization program. Its goal was to work among the black community in Gary to interest the black man in taking over his own affairs. Community organization was understood as a means by which citizens in a democratic social order participate in political, economic, social, and cultural decision-making.

By November, 1967, the Inner City Task Force had brought together the representatives of six indigenous groups from the inner city. Other organizations and gangs were encouraged to join in order to lay the foundation for a mass-based indigenous community organization. According to plans for the next step, a program would be initiated to train responsive persons from the black community in the techniques of community organization. In addition, the Inner City Task Force has approached some denominations to make funds available for the employment of a highly skilled community organizer who would be in charge of the training program.

In Gary ministers and concerned laymen use the model of a nonprofessional community organization as a device to deal effectively with poverty structures. This kind of activity is functional mission because it uses skillful methods for the expression of the church's commitment to people in need. According to a report from the Inner City Task Force, the overall goal is this: "We cannot decide for the men and women of mid-town; they must make the decision, plan the action and reap the benefits or losses of such action. We can only act as a catalyst, an advisor or consultant."

An illustration for the second type, the involvement of the church in a professional community organization, is the *Organization for the Southwest Community* (*OSC*) *in Chicago.* This project was started when in 1959 over 1,000 delegates from 104 churches, civic associations, PTA groups, lodges, and other organizations came together for the first meeting. A statement about the purpose says, "We decided to act: 1) why people were departing from such a splendidly equipped community, 2) to solve the problems that caused people to move, and 3) to get them to stay in the community." [2] The question arises, What has been the role of the church in such an approach to solving community problems? Although this model does not deal with poverty structures predominantly, it nevertheless can demonstrate the form of church involvement in an efficient organization, the idea and structure of which was applied to community problems at so many other places.

The driving cause behind the concern in Chicago was the expanding Negro ghetto. To deal most efficiently with the complex situation on the Southwest side of Chicago, Saul Alinsky's Industrial Areas Foundation, a training institute for community organizers and a catalyst for starting particular community organizations, was called to the area in 1959. Although only about fifteen churches participated fully in OSC, many others showing no concern whatsoever, their contribution is regarded to be basic for the growth of OSC over the years. The role of the churches was three-fold: (1) They provided most of the financial support necessary to maintain a professionally staffed organization. (2) They provided an effective channel of communication by which committee personnel could be recruited and information conveyed. (3) Most important of all, they provided leaders who, in coalition with other civic leaders, were able to shape the policy and direction of OSC.

[2] *The Edge of the Ghetto,* ed. by John Fisk, *et al.* (Chicago: The University of Chicago Press, 1966), p. 1.

169

11
Functional Mission to Free Time Structures

In an earlier chapter it was said that the wholeness
of human life in contemporary technological society is determined by three major functions: working, living (in any
residential sector), and celebrating. The first two were examined according to their importance for the development
of specialized ministries. It is the goal of this final chapter
to deal with the third. What forms have been developed
by ministers and laymen to carry on functional mission in
man's leisure time? Before attempting an answer three
general aspects should be considered.

1) Structural. No other term appears to fit better than
the phrase "presence structures" to characterize functional
mission to the world of leisure. Many ministers who work
in this field speak of the "ministry of the being-here." The
theologically trained reader will recognize immediately that
this terminology is used by existentialist theologians. Indeed, mission in this area may be signified as the kerygma-
tic application of an existentialist-influenced theology. To
be "present" in mission means to be where points of correlation for the church in mass communication emerge today.
This leads to the second point.

2) Geographical. The shopping center, the coffeehouse,
the campground, or the bar are places where the paths of
many people cross each other today. At those places, the

ministry of the being-here assumes temporarily firm forms. In this situation the search for proper correlation points becomes utterly important. Two possibilities may be identified: (1) geographically fixed mission where the missionary has chosen a fixed place that serves as starting point for his work, for instance, a storefront; (2) sporadic mission where high mobility has not yet allowed, or never will, the setting up of a geographically fixed location. As a result, the missionary is permanently on the move. The night minister is a pertinent illustration of this type.

3) Functional-correlative. In systematic theology Paul Tillich's method was determined by the search for the correlation point of religion and life. Likewise, the theologian in charge of any form of functional mission tries to find the correlation point of religion and life style. Conversely, the form in which he performs mission is determined by specific behavioral attitudes during leisure time. To find this missionary correlation point is *the* task in this field.

GEOGRAPHICALLY FIXED MINISTRY

1. THE COFFEEHOUSE MINISTRY. The coffeehouse ministry is the only one so far that has been a subject for systematic research. Study of it has even resulted in a book.[1] An additional flood of literature documents the popularity of this type of functional mission. Without downgrading other successful experiments, it may be said that the coffeehouse ministry is the most copied new form of ministry these days. One can even speak of a coffeehouse movement in which, by 1966, more than 1,000 projects were known.[2] This coffeehouse ministry started with two structural novelties back in the fifties.

The first was the *Bread and Wine Mission in San Francisco*, with the intention of ministry to the artistic com-

---

[1] John D. Perry, *The Coffee House Ministry* (Richmond, Va.: John Knox Press, 1966).

[2] *Ibid.,* p. 19.

munity of North Beach. This project was inaugurated by the Congregationalists in June, 1958. The minister who was in charge of the Bread and Wine Mission in the first years rented a storefront and invited the beatniks to use the room as a forum. Another important step was taken when his successor offered his apartment for informal chats with members of the artistic community. There his young friends sat on mats anxious to enter into dialogue with the missionary. The second was the Potter's House,[3] a project begun by the Church of the Saviour in Washington, D.C., in 1960.

From the very beginning the coffeehouse had a specific constituency, more sophisticated in composition than any other experiment of functional mission. At present three major types of coffeehouses may be identified: (1) the urban adult coffeehouse, (2) the campus coffeehouse, (3) the teen-canteen coffeehouse. While the urban adult and campus coffeehouses attract primarily higher educated persons in the late teens and the twenties, the third type, the teen-canteen, has as its purpose to minister to street youngsters. The teen-canteen coffeehouse came into existence during the riots of 1964 in New York. The teen-canteen also appeals—in contrast to the two previous ones —strongly to youngsters from lower-class families. Since the teen-canteen, with its predominantly social-work structure, must be regarded as a vehicle for the promotion of already existing programs, it lacks the experimental spirit of those coffeehouses that work more with intellectuals. My further account, therefore, is confined to this latter type.

Almost every manager of a coffeehouse emphasizes dialogue in various forms as the major purpose for its existence, or as Perry puts it, "The coffee house provides an opportunity to experience dialogue, not just to talk about it." [4] Simultaneously, the coffeehouse is a test laboratory for the

[3] See p. 50.
[4] *The Coffee House Ministry*, p. 45.

idea held by some that dialogue is one of the last possibilities that can help to revive the church. Indeed, the coffeehouse is the proper place to involve youth and young adults in discussions about religion. Despisers of the coffeehouse notwithstanding, it can be said today that the coffeehouse is one of the few new forms of ministry that has been successful in finding a correlation point in functional mission to the young intellectual. Questionnaires show that the coffeehouse is for many the only place where unchurched young adults start to talk again about religion. When the "Precarious Vision" in San Francisco still was in operation, an opinion poll was taken there in 1965. It turned out that 57 percent of those present had not been to church during the last month before the poll. Fifty-one percent had not been to church during the six months before, and 38 percent had not attended any worship service during the previous year.[5]

Most coffeehouses are located in former storefronts. *The Door* in Chicago, for instance, is easily identifiable as a place where religion is not sold in a closed package, but has to be experienced in the informal atmosphere of dialogue and discussion groups. The person who visits the Door passes through a small book display before he reaches the tables and stools in the back of the storefront. The combination of bookstore and coffeehouse has not only economic reasons, but expresses the uniqueness of this missionary structure—the coffeehouse is primarily a contemporary medium in the communication process of the church with the world. It amplifies the message of the church to the people who could never be addressed in a more effective way elsewhere. The coffeehouse has proved to be the young adult medium of the church.

The missionary structure of the coffeehouse is also determined by the willingness on the side of the church to *serve*. By the same token the church sacrifices its brick and stone structures to coffeehouses located in former

---

[5] From a paper, "Interpretation of a Questionnaire Given to the Clientele of the Precarious Vision" by Keith McCrary, April, 1965.

supermarkets, laundromats, art print stores, and taverns. Furthermore, it "declericalizes" its personnel. As a result, with the growing popularity of the coffeehous idea, the layman got his great chance. Perry writes, "The coffee house movement provides an excellent experimental situation for the whole church to explore the implications of the new theology of the laity." [6]

As a matter of fact, the clergyman is equal to his unordained brother in the coffeehouse; he participates in its activities just like everybody else. Hence, the coffeehouse ministry is one of the few types of functional mission where the layman has assumed major responsibilities. He does not simply serve coffee, he also enables conversations, coordinates discussion groups, and asks important questions. In the coffeehouse the layman has taken over the position the clergyman occupied in the church.

There are coffeehouses that offer a very structured program. Features may be poetry readings, painting and other artistic presentations, musical presentations, dramatic presentations and play readings, folk and freedom songs, and lectures or discussions. Many names breathe the experimental spirit of their sponsors and managers: *The Edge,* in Bryn Mawr, Pennsylvania; *The Threshing Floor,* in Greenwich Village; and the *Precarious Vision,* a former coffeehouse in San Francisco.

Le Rapport, in Seattle, Washington, opened in 1963. About one-half of the financial support comes from individual gifts.[7] This coffeehouse is located next to a movie theater. Although it has economic difficulties, managers and clientele are happy that Le Rapport has no official connection with the church. This coffeehouse is visited by young businessmen, professionals, and graduate students alike. Back in 1966 the number of participants varied between 25 and 200. Most of the discussions used to begin on weekend evenings at 10:00 P.M. and continue into the

[6] *The Coffee House Ministry,* p. 39.
[7] For this and other data see *Encounter,* quarterly magazine of Christian Theological Seminary, Autumn, 1966, p. 312.

early morning hours. Here are some of the current discussion subjects: civil rights; liturgical jazz; sex, love, and meaning; existentialism; disarmament; political conservatism; Bertrand Russell and Christianity; the Bible and modern science; James Baldwin; and Ingmar Bergman's theological trilogy. Once in a while, discussions are led by outstanding leaders from the state and community. They usually begin with a brief introduction to an issue followed by a question and answer period.

More frequented by students and less structured in its program is *The Cracked Cup* in Columbus, Ohio, which has operated since 1966. "It's beautiful," one young man from California said enthusiastically. "It's what I've always wished that a coffeehouse could be, and I've been in lots of them." The walls covered with reproductions of modern paintings, this coffeehouse, initiated by Dave Dunning, a young minister of Trinity Episcopal Church, has a small stage where folk singers express their feelings to the young people attentively listening. Lemon tea and espresso go for ten cents; chips, pretzels, and fritos for fifty cents. When the last sound of protest songs has died away, explosive topics provide a solid basis for discussions. These young adults know that the Cracked Cup is a place of freedom to explore the depth dimension in human life. One of the sponsors expressed recently what could be said vicariously for the other 1,000 coffeehouses: "A skeptic, agnostic, or critic can participate in the coffeehouse without first giving in or up. ... At the same time the church can listen." [8]

2. GANG MINISTRY. As mentioned, functional mission to youth and young adults addresses two different groups of persons: (1) the higher educated and better-off youngsters, and (2) the less educated street gangs. The former are predominantly "served" by the Christian coffeehouse, the latter have challenged the churches to invent forms of ministry that are appropriate to their life style. There are various ways to help youngsters who are simply hang-

[8] *The Columbus Dispatch,* Sunday magazine, April 9, 1967, p. 47.

175

ing around. One type of gang ministry came into existence in Chicago not too long ago. It cannot claim, however, to represent all other types; yet, it can show what a gang ministry looks like.

Park Manor Youth Center, initiated by Park Manor Christian Church is located in a storefront and offers programs of recreational activities, education, job finding, and counseling. This recreational, counseling, and informative function shapes the form of this kind of ministry. It does not reach from geographically fixed headquarters to those who came through their own initiative or who accidentally can be contacted somewhere in the area. Hence, the program is geared to meet the elementary needs of youngsters, not just to fulfill their intellectual expectations in the area of religion, as is the case with the coffeehouse ministry. These gang members need advice in life situations that the coffeehouse clientele usually need not be concerned about.

James E. Kohls, who works with gangs in Chicago, once said, "This is the only project I know of which has the interest and involvement of the total community." This statement is the more surprising since the neighborhood of Park Manor is the scene of extensive gang violence. Mr. Kohls first tried to bring gangs to the church. But that did not work. When they met with youngsters from an active youth group that already existed, fights broke out and windows were broken out of the church. This disappointing experience forced the youth leader to admit that something else had to be done.

As violence increased, with gangs shooting from cars, Kohls began to interest the community in a youth center. Finally several churches, a great number of businessmen, industries, and civic groups could be involved to share the expenses of the youth center. The Youth Council, as this ministry is also called, has a general board that makes the overall decisions and guides the direction of the program. It is composed of five adults and five teen-agers. One of the older persons had this to say: "It's wonderful to see these kids begin to work for themselves. Now they are beginning to feel that they have a place in this community, that they have friends among the businessmen and church people who they thought were their enemies before." This type of ministry may not yield an impressive theology of mission. But it has changed the relation between the community and militant young people for the better.

Apart from the two types of youth ministry mentioned, there are many others. San Francisco, for instance, has some outstanding projects, such as the Young Adult Center and the Young Adult Project. The latter was a nationwide approach to minister to young people with its headquarters in Nashville, Tennessee.[9] But a report at length about this aspect of functional mission would fill another book. Instead, we turn now to another form of free time ministry.

SPORADIC MISSION

Contemporary man does not spend his free time at geographically fixed places only. Often he pursues a nomadic life style, rushing from place to place, seeking a few hours of relaxation and fun, and then all at once is on the run again. The church has responded to this life style with the development of what may be called sporadic mission. The missionary, accordingly, is permanently on the move; he is where the people are. One is almost tempted to say he is not ministering to their needs, but to their mobility.

1. THE NIGHT MINISTRY. The Reverend Donald Stuart, who is in charge of the *Night Ministry in San Francisco* is perhaps the most reported about minister throughout the country. He serves in one of the most thrilling and demanding ministries his denomination—the United Church of Christ—has to offer. "San Francisco is a lonely city," the forty-two-year-old married minister said. "Transients and single persons come here from all over the country. They come seeking companionship, perhaps a new life.

[9] See *The Methodist Story* magazine, April, 1968, pp. 14-15.

Many don't find either. I can share their loneliness. The relationships I form are seldom lasting ones. I may know someone almost intimately for a couple of hours. Then they are gone—sort of gobbled up by the night." There are no pews, no hymnbooks, no chimes, and no pulpit in this ministry. But there is the wandering, restless congregation of prostitutes, homosexuals, bartenders, taxi drivers, and hotel clerks.

Stuart's parish includes the Tenderloin area in downtown San Francisco, hotel lobbies, the bus terminal, numerous cafeterias and bars, and apartments where desperate persons attempt suicide. Night after night this scenery is the shape of Stuart's ministry. As a matter of fact, San Francisco has one of the highest suicide rates in the country, and even in the world. The night minister does not know only the beauty of that city with the Golden Gate Bridge and the Japanese Garden; he also is confronted with the anxieties and outcries of residents in nocturnal San Francisco. "Their depression and loneliness seem to focus in the night hours. If we can help them through the darkness —just till dawn when life becomes less frightening—they usually can endure another day," the night minister comments. What is the structure of a night ministry to people with such an "unstructured" life?

The night ministry in San Francisco is a combined service involving a clergyman, an associate, and several laymen who man the telephone during the night hours. This ministry is a cross between a suicide prevention and a mobile counseling service. It is characterized by the "wandering minister," patrolling the streets of downtown San Francisco, keeping himself alert for needs, and providing help in any form. Set up in 1964, this project is sponsored by seven denominations through the San Francisco Council of Churches.

Don Stuart, the night minister, resumes his duty when his colleagues, the day ministers, are about to go to bed. Around 10:00 P.M. a tall man with a clerical collar enters Sam's Hofbrau, a twenty-four-hour cafeteria. He is known here. A youngster, hanging around at the bar, greets him with "Hi, Don." Another patron, alone with himself and a glass of beer, gets an encouraging word from Stuart. Later, he explained that this man has a drinking problem. He is one of those "members" in Stuart's "congregation" who needs counseling badly. The night minister is the right man to do that. Sam's Hofbrau is Stuart's headquarters, so to speak. From here he starts his nocturnal patrols through downtown San Francisco, and here he will return two or three hours later.

What Stuart needs most on duty, he has—oddly enough —in his pockets. In one he always keeps some extra dimes for urgent telephone calls; in the other pocket he carries a tiny beeper. One night when he sat in a hotel lobby chatting with the clerk the beeper began to beep. This meant that he was wanted by his telephone volunteers. Once the beeper starts beeping, the night minister goes to the nearest available telephone and calls his two associates manning the phone. Sixty volunteers are available, of whom two are on duty each night. When somebody in San Francisco dials 621-8282 from 10:00 P.M. to 6:00 A.M. one of these volunteers answers the phone, "Night ministry. May I help you?" He then is ready to listen and to deal with every problem. If the case proves to be too difficult, he transfers to Don Stuart, reaching him through the little beeper. He then continues the conversation over the phone.

This was the case one night when Stuart sat in the hotel lobby. He immediately called his volunteers and learned that a distraught mother of four young children had called 621-8282 for help. Hysterically, she told on the phone that she was killing herself and her children. But she did not want to give her address. A critical period came when the volunteer tried to keep her on the line while his colleague worked feverishly with the operator to find out her location. The woman hung up without giving her address. But she did not know that the operator had probably done the best job in his life. Stuart sent the police and rushed there himself. The officers broke through the barricaded door

179

and found the house filled with gas and the children unconscious. All were taken to the hospital and saved. Stuart's comment at the end of this hectic night was, "One call and the budget for the entire year is made worthwhile."

When Mr. Stuart was back again on his nocturnal patrol, a stoop-shouldered, unshaven man croaked hoarsely, "May I speak to you alone, Father?" Then, for a quarter of an hour, the night minister took him aside, and, slowly walking, they entered a counseling session.

Then there was a man from Oakland who called in desperation one night threatening suicide. He was an alcoholic. Stuart talked to him for more than two hours. Two months later, a man approached Stuart on Mason Street and identified himself as the one he had talked to for so long on the phone. He said he had not had a drink since that night and was now an active member of A.A.

Stuart knows how to find out about the needs of his clients. "These people aren't oddballs or freaks. It's just that their identity has taken a form normally rejected by society. They don't erect barriers to mask their emotions. So you see them as they are. And at first it looks like another world."

But a night minister must have sleep, too. Stuart has arranged to rest from 6:30 A.M. to 11:30 A.M. and from 2:30 P.M. to 5:30 P.M. Although he has two days off a week, the stress of this ministry is tremendous. This becomes apparent when the night minister sits down for a moment in a coffeehouse at North Beach at 4:00 A.M. According to Stuart's own words, "The emotional strain and constant tension when the beeper goes off remains my greatest occupational hazard." But nevertheless he likes this demanding job. The great personal sacrifices notwithstanding, he wants to spend more years in this ministry. Once a week he meets with psychiatrists to discuss case material. As far as his future plans are concerned, he intends to gather a worshiping congregation that would meet between two and three o'clock in the morning in the lobby of one of San Francisco's hotels. Until then, Mr. Stuart will work in a structure he has shaped alone. "I refuse to allow my relationships to be anything more than clinical. When this happens, the pastoral nature of this ministry will be lost."

2. MINISTRY TO RECREATIONAL RESORTS. Free time in America, as anywhere in the world, is spent on a short-span and a long-span basis. Short-span free time is spent in the bars, houses, and on the streets. Long-span free time is spent apart from the polluted city air, somewhere in the mountains or on the beach. Statistics show how attractive, for instance, ski vacations have become within recent years. More than three million Americans are skiing annually. According to *Sports Illustrated* [10] more than 10 percent of Seattle's population take to the hills regularly for skiing. A study by the Outdoor Recreation Resources Review Commission (Rockefeller Commission) concluded that "outdoor recreation activity, already a major part of American life, will triple by the year 2000." And the report goes on, stating, "Outdoor activity, whether undertaken lightly or with serious intent . . . is essentially a renewing experience. . . . The fact that we live in a world that moves crisis by crisis does not make a growing interest in outdoor activities frivolous or ample provisions for them unworthy of the nation's concern." Hence, the Reverend Donald L. Baldwin, ski chaplain in California's Yosemite National Park, when asked by a skier standing next to him on a slope if he really thinks the church ought to be in these recreational areas, answered, "My only response is that the church *cannot* afford *not* to be!"

Don Baldwin, like many of his colleagues in this field of functional mission, serves in a combined geographically fixed and sporadic ministry. Mr. Baldwin holds as his primary job the pastorate of the interdenominational *Yosemite Community Church*. In addition, on winter Sundays after the regular worship service there, he hightails it to the Badger Pass ski area eighteen miles away where he conducts an outdoor service for skiers. Such a worship hour

[10] January 6, 1964.

181

on the slope may draw as many as sixty skiers out of more than three thousand visitors on weekends. In order to worship they form a semicircle around the minister, face a big cross stuck into the snow, identifying the spot as a temporary Christian worship place, as a church without roof, pews, or pulpits.

Besides conducting worship, the minister in recreational resorts becomes more and more a counselor. Asked for a comment on this aspect of his service, Baldwin said, "Many are either running or searching, and they think that somehow in the mountains they may begin to find themselves. When they don't, there's general discouragement, and that's where my counseling ministry comes in." [11]

Colorado, the other great ski resort area, has three world famous sport centers—Aspen, Vail, and Snowmass. Into two of them, Vail and Snowmass, the Lutheran Church of America has sent ministers. In Snowmass, the Reverend Lee Healy, a forty-two-year-old Pennsylvanian, took over his responsibilities. The Board of American Mission bought a $15,000 studio apartment as a base of operation. The living room is big enough to hold informal services for twenty. The cross, put on an ordinary table, is fashioned from ski tips. Worship there is open for any kind of spontaneity. Frequently a guitar player will accompany the singing. The service ends when the cable car begins running. Quite accidentally Mr. Healy learned from several visitors what had become apparent on other occasions, too—that the leadership of the church is much more versatile and liberal than the members. Says Healy, "They think it's great that we're interested enough to come in here. But at the same time they still expect the church to stick to its traditional forms. When we bring in a guitarist or sing folk songs, they're shocked." [12]

Together with his colleague Don Simonton—the other chaplain in this area, who was called to Vail—Mr. Healy

[11] *Together* magazine, February, 1967, p. 37.
[12] Robert E. Huldschiner, "Pasters to the Ski Crowd," *The Lutheran* magazine, March 27, 1968, p. 10.

forms the *High County Lutheran Parish,* which operates between the residents and the skiers. Besides the early Sunday morning service, they hold church school on Mondays (Sundays proved to be inconvenient because of ski competitions) and a Sunday evening program featuring films and discussions.

The rest of the time these two ministers are on the slope pursuing their sporadic ministry. Their goal is to be available, to be with the people. Don Simonton tells of a letter he received from a participant in a morning service. According to this letter, the girl, stunned by the recent death of her father, returned to the slopes that morning with a new outlook on life. "I've made my best contacts on the slopes," pastor Simonton says.

People who ride up with me on the chairlift are relaxed, introspective. . . . They may suddenly spill out their problems —a love affair, friction with their parents. They figure they can talk to me. Often I can meet them later in the evening and help them straighten things out. Of course, I'll never know what comes of it. The results may not show for ten years, and then a thousand miles away. A few words exchanged on the slope or on the lift may be the delayed-reaction trigger for an insight into what the church is all about.[13]

One of the surprising results of the ministry to recreational resorts is that lay people show a rather strong feeling of dependency upon a church building. The ski ministry has made it clear why experimental ministries without a church building have to struggle so hard in areas other than leisure and recreation. The $50,000 chapel of St. Bernard in the Snoqualmie mountains near Seattle, to be sure, has pleased many visitors, but has caused a lot of critical remarks from church leaders. A report on this ministry says bluntly, "In the minds of the laymen at least, it (the chapel) tends to solidify the ministry of the church as being building-oriented and building-centered.[14] Or Don Simonton reports the feeling of Vail skiers in these words,

[13] *Ibid.*
[14] Report released by the Diocese of Olympia, Washington.

"They can't get rid of the notion that the church is a build-ing with a cross on top. They'd love a real church in Vail—like frosting on a cake—a nice steeple to round out the picture. When I tell them that the church is people and program before it's pews, they stare." [15]

Sporadic ministries are not reserved for recreational re-sorts in the mountains only. The beach is a challenge, too. This is what two seminarians from Concordia Seminary in St. Louis thought. Robert and Donald Dretzschmar traveled in the summer of 1966 at the invitation of a church board to *Ocean City, Maryland,* in order to perform an *experimental beach ministry,* as they called it. Instead of preaching with words only, they sang the gospel on their guitars. Since many teen-agers come to this summer resort to get jobs in the flourishing tourist business, Ocean City is an especially rewarding place for a ministry like this. These youngsters used to spend their time off on the beach, which is famous as one of the widest, most beautiful beach-es on the Atlantic.

The Kretzschmar brothers soon found out that there was no real opportunity for teen-agers to enjoy meaningful leisure time. Ocean City operates seven days a week, and many teen-agers with jobs could not attend any church service. The two seminarians jumped into this breach. For one summer they showed up here and there on the beach, replacing the pulpit with the bandshell, the robe with swim-ming trunks, and the litany with folk songs. The response was overwhelming. These modern gospel singers attracted a spontaneous audience of seventy-five teen-agers or more.

Contacts on the glimmering beach were made easily. Part of the audience usually stayed to talk after the twin brothers finished singing. As the Kretzschmars remarked after their summer experience, "In conversing with them we gained some good friendships and could share Christ more personally with individuals. These were some experiences we won't forget." On Tuesdays and Thursdays, in addition,

[15] *The Lutheran* magazine, p. 10.

they got together with friends they met in town for worship and fellowship. As the two evangelists say, their experiences with the experimental beach ministry "were sources of strength for us. Hearing and sharing the faith of these others was great. Here we could receive as well as give."

CONCLUSION

THE ACTION-THEOLOGY ASPECT

The analysis of the structures of missionary congregations and of the styles of functional mission has shown the high flexibility of a number of churches and individuals. While the majority of clergymen still prefer to keep the Babylonian captivity of the church alive behind the walls of a pre-technological society, an avant-garde of ministers and laymen has attracted wide attention. It stands for a "theology of action," the central message of which is God *is* mission; God is not simply sending his missionaries into the world. Hence, these avant-garde ministers push aside every "Gestalt"-form in the church which they believe is in the way of God's action in this world. Quite a number of these experiment-oriented ministers and laymen even claim that the presence of a church building jeopardizes the missionary mobility of the church.

Most experiments may be characterized as "ventures in social ethics." Simultaneously, something like the political pastor and the political congregation arises. "Political" is used here in the light of a new theology of mission. According to this concept, the congregation no longer remains in the realm of individual piety, but takes part in God's public action. The implications for the structure are considerable. The congregation seeks an exodus into the world; it appears at those places where society needs its reconciliatory function most. As the analyses of American parishes and extra-parochial activities have shown, the church becomes "political" once it can make a contribution to the solution of social problems. In the case of Glide Memorial Methodist Church in San Francisco[1] the principle of action is that the construction of the congregation is also the construction of the urban society.

THE ICONOCLASTIC ASPECT

Church renewal is in its most general sense a structural protest against institutionalism. In this respect, it has iconoclastic significance. Gabriel Vahanian in his book *Wait Without Idols* has written, "Iconoclasm is, for all practical purposes, the essential ingredient of monotheism as understood in the biblical tradition. Without this element, faith in God loses its indispensable character, and can result neither in radical commitment to God nor in an equally radical and iconoclastic involvement in the world."[2] Along with Vahanian, many theologians criticize traditional church life as a dance around the Golden Calf. They act instead as iconoclasts. They set the macro-structures of the institutional church against the micro-structures of the church in the diaspora. The formation of the "left wing" of the First Congregational Church in Elmhust[3] is a classical example of the fact that a congregation has rejuvenated itself in an iconoclastic way. Iconoclasm applied to church renewal signifies that revolutionary process in which the traditional "come" structure is replaced by the "go" structure.

Simultaneously, the tendency for uncompromising experimentation has become apparent because the meaning of "community" in the church has become gloomy and nebulous. Some avant-garde persons have a remarkable alternative—the study group of concerned Christians who live and work under a self-imposed discipline. Here the

[1] Pp. 76-81.
[2] (New York: George Braziller, 1964), p. 26.
[3] P. 43.

all-important *outer* structure of the traditional congregation is replaced in favor of a strict discipline *within* the small groups: the Church of the Saviour in Washington, D.C., the Ecumenical Institute in Chicago, and the East Harlem Protestant Parish in New York, where ministers originally have accepted a common discipline in living and working.

THE EXPERIMENTAL ASPECT

Perhaps the most original contribution of American church life to the renewal discussion in the oekumene is the discovery of the experiment as a mark of the contemporary church. Some ministers and laymen have made it clear that experimentation with new church structures is no transitory phenomenon or, even worse, a necessary modernistic concession to changes in society in order to attract modern man. Quite the contrary is true. The readiness for experimentation grows out of a careful theoretical preparatory activity, and leads from the action-oriented theology, via iconoclasm, to experiment as the life style of the church in the second half of the twentieth century. According to action-oriented theology, the congregation is never prior to her members who want to act through her. Instead, the people are prior and make her to become public through experimental forms. Unfortunately, the bias against the word "experiment" is still considerable among many theologians and church members. But it is hoped that the presentation of facts, as offered in this book, may lead the critics to concede that it was the experiment—and the experiment only—that gave back to the church vigor and strength to respond to the revolutionary changes in society. The experiment in the church no longer proves to be something provisional in the negative sense, but has become a structural imperative. Perhaps we are ready at the end of this decade to have the courage to experiment with new forms as a ministerial prerequisite. A look at the constructive unrest in the church, of which this book hopes to be a witness, makes us ask if "vita experimentalis" is not the contribution of God's wandering people for the last third of this century.

THE MISSIONARY ASPECT

The structures of the congregation are not the only things subject to experimentation. The concept of mission has undergone a drastic change, too. What was described in the second part of this book as *functional mission* is nothing else than the attempt to expose mission to growing specialization in all areas of life. Mission is no longer the universal key that matches each door of our different departments in society. Instead, each door gets its own key, since society has put additional safety locks on its doors. Thanks to the development of a great variety of specialized ministries, the church today has a whole bunch of keys that can fit each single one of these doors.

At present the avant-garde in the church holds that mission is the specialized function of the church in differentiated areas of modern society. The example of the Ecumenical Associates in Lansing[4] demonstrates impressively that mission today can no longer start with the proclamation of the kerygma—no matter *how* enthusiastic—but is compelled to answer, first of all, the question, In what degree shall mission be specialized if it wants to open the numerous doors of our differentiated society for the Good News?

In this connection new light is shed on the old dualism of parochial–nonparochial. The social sciences have sufficiently shown that contemporary man can no longer be reached for social development exclusively at his place of residence. Accordingly, the residential parish is suffering from a sociological narrowness as long as it is concerned with the residential sectors only. In this situation an interesting solution seems to be at hand. It proves that parochial

4 P. 160.

and nonparochial functions stand necessarily in a mutual relationship.

The combination of both areas—parochial and extra-parochial—has its roots not in the fact that some ministers are ecumenically open, but in the fact that the sociology of modern society makes integration imperative. One might ask, Why combine these two realms? Because many people can be reached by the church only in these specific areas of function, which are usually outside the congregation. This means that in the future the local parish in its recruitment of members will be dependent upon specialized, extra-parochial ministries. The missionary in a special assignment, on the other hand, is led by the assurance that he can send people interested in church life to a local congregation where a community will still be intact. And finally, should we not cease to think in geographical categories— "parochial–extra-parochial?" Instead, we should learn to think in functional terms—that is, any church life in the future should be characterized by the mutuality between the "missionary structure of the *congregation*" and *"functional mission* in society."

THE COOPERATIONAL ASPECT

East Harlem Protestant Parish would not have been kept alive without the cooperation between the three ministers (at least in the initial stage); the Church of the Saviour in Washington could not have obtained its wide reputation in the ecumenical movement without the close relationship between the minister and the members of the congregation. In view of the great responsibility the church has for society, cooperation on any level is the prerequisite for successful church work. Or to put it negatively, the ecclesiastical egocentricity that upsets every cooperation condemns the church to harmlessness and irrelevance.

Right now the most massive administrative expression for cooperation is the merger of several congregations into one parish. The example of the West St. Louis Ecumenical

Parish[5] shows that the impact of the church program on the community after the merger is incomparably more effective. For the first time people in that community got to know that the church still exists. Interestingly enough, the tendency to cooperate was intensified by the rapid urbanization of America. In the context of the city, this principle has become almost a credo: The city can be mastered theologically only if congregations work together on any potential level. Behind this concept there is the conviction of the reformer that urbanization requires a kind of working style that takes the *whole* of the city into consideration, not only—as was true in the past—small sectors. This is one of the reasons why the denominations are occupied now with the elaboration of strategies for modern urban church work.

What is ahead for the church? "The church in experiment," the new structural expression of a Christian lifestyle adventure for the last third of the twentieth century.

[5] P. 83.

BIBLIOGRAPHY

I. MISSION IN GENERAL

The Church for Others and the Church for the World. Final Report of the Western European Working Group and North American Working Group of the Department on Studies in Evangelism. Geneva: World Council of Churches, 1967.

Hoekendijk, J. C. *The Church Inside Out.* Philadelphia: Westminster Press, 1966.

Margull, Hans J. *Hope in Action: The Church's Task in the World.* Philadelphia: Muhlenberg Press, 1962.

Osborn, Ronald E. *In Christ's Place. Christian Ministry in Today's World.* St. Louis: Bethany Press, 1967.

Raines, Robert. *The Secular Congregation.* New York: Harper, 1968.

Walker, Alan. *A Ringing Call to Mission.* Nashville: Abingdon Press, 1966.

Wieser, Thomas, ed. *Planning for Mission.* New York: World Council of Churches, 1966.

Williams, Colin W. *What in the World?* New York: National Council of Churches, 1964.

————. *Where in the World?* New York: National Council of Churches, 1963.

II. CASE STUDIES AND REPORTS ON EXPERIMENTAL FORMS OF MINISTRY

Boyd, Malcolm, ed. *The Underground Church.* New York: Sheed & Ward, 1968.

Casteel, John L. *The Creative Role of Interpersonal Groups in the Church Today.* New York: Association Press, 1968. Thirteen accounts of various small group programs.

Clark, Edward, et al. *The Church Creative: A Reader on the Renewal of the Church.* Nashville: Abingdon Press, 1967.

Fackre, Gabriel. "The Crisis of the Congregation," in *Voluntary Associations: Essays in Honor of James Luther Adams.*

193

Richmond, Va.: John Knox Press, 1966, pp. 276-97. This is an introductory article of high quality with an excellent bibliography of 86 items.

Goodman, Grace Ann. *The Church and the Apartment House.* Published by the United Presbyterian Church in the U.S.A.

———. *Rocking the Ark.* New York: Presbyterian Distribution Service, 1969. Nine case studies of congregations of from 100 to 3,000 members in rural, downtown, and suburban locations.

Halvorson, Lawrence W. *The Church in a Diverse Society.* Minneapolis: Augsburg, 1964. Case studies on the work of churches with minority groups and other important sociological segments of American society.

Kenrick, Bruce. *Come out the Wilderness. The Story of the East Harlem Protestant Parish.* New York: Harper, 1962.

Metz, Donald L. *New Congregations.* Philadelphia: Westminster Press, 1967. A study of new Protestant congregations designed to suggest hypotheses about the factors affecting the course of development of new churches.

Moore, Richard E., and Day, Duane L. *Urban Church Breakthrough.* New York: Harper, 1966. First major attempt to conceptualize current phenomena of church renewal.

Myers, C. Kilmer. *Light the Dark Streets.* New York: Seabury Press, 1957. This is the Episcopal equivalent to George W. Webber's books. Myers describes his service as a vicar of the Lower Eastside Mission of Trinity Parish in New York.

O'Connor, Elizabeth. *Call to Commitment: The Story of the Church of the Saviour in Washington, D.C.* New York: Harper, 1963.

Perry, John D. *The Coffee House Ministry.* Richmond, Va.: John Knox Press, 1966.

Raines, Robert A. *New Life in the Church.* New York: Harper, 1961. This is about Raines's experience with the small group approach in Aldersgate Methodist Church in Cleveland, Ohio.

Sills, Horace S., ed. *Grassroots Ecumenicity. Case Studies in Local Church Consolidation.* Philadelphia: United Church Press, 1967. Six case studies about United Church of Christ congregations that were involved in mergers with churches from other denominations.

Stagg, Paul L. *The Converted Church.* Valley Forge, Pa.: Judson Press, 1967. Chapter 4, "Ventures in Missionary Obedience," analyzes several experiments.

Webber, George W. *God's Colony in Man's World.* Nashville: Abingdon Press, 1960.

———. *The Congregation in Mission.* Nashville: Abingdon Press, 1964. Both of Webber's books deal with the East Harlem Protestant Parish in New York, founded in 1948.

III. PERIODICALS THAT REGULARLY REPORT ON CHURCH RENEWAL

Church in Metropolis (the Episcopal Church). 475 Riverside Drive, New York, N.Y. 10027.
The Lutheran (the Lutheran Church in America). 2900 Queen Lane, Philadelphia, Pa. 19129
The Methodist Story. 1200 Davis Street, Evanston, Ill. 60201
Presbyterian Life. Witherspoon Building, Philadelphia, Pa. 19107
Renewal (Interdenominational). 116 South Michigan, Chicago, Ill. 60603
United Church Herald (United Church of Christ), Box 7095, St. Louis, Mo. 63177

IV. READING MATERIAL ON CONGREGATIONS AND SPECIALIZED MINISTRIES DEALT WITH IN THIS BOOK

Agora Shopping Center Ministry in Oakbrook, Ill.
   Reader's Digest, June, 1966.
Apartment-House Ministry
   "Skymarks." An Analysis and Prognosis of the High-rise Luxury Apartment as a Context for the Ministry. Distributed by the Board of National Missions, Presbyterian Church in the U.S.A., 475 Riverside Drive, New York, N.Y.
   Grace Ann Goodman, *The Church and the Apartment House.*
   Christian Century, May 10, 1967, pp. 615-17.
   World Outlook magazine, February, 1965, pp. 10-13.
   Clark, *et al., The Church Creative,* pp. 169-77.
   Lee, *Cities and Churches,* pp. 116-24.
Broadway Methodist Church in Indianapolis
   Together magazine, October, 1967, pp. 50-55
Christ Church Presbyterian in Burlington, Vt.
   The Church for Others, pp. 95-98, 127-29
   Presbyterian Life, April 1, 1961.
   International Journal of Religious Education, September, 1965, pp. 4-5.
   Grace Ann Goodman, *The Pilgrimage of Christ Church Presbyterian* (Board of National Missions, United Presbyterian Church in the U.S.A., 1967).
   Clark, *et al., The Church Creative,* pp. 140-53.

Church and Community Organization
  The Church for Others, pp. 113-16
  Renewal, January, 1967, pp. 11-13, 16-18
  Moore and Day, *Urban Church Breakthrough*, p. 63.
  The Church in Urban America. A Resource Book for the Methodist Fourth Quadrenniel Convention on Urban Life in America, 1966, pp. 109-19.
  The Church in Metropolis magazine, special issue on church and community organization, summer, 1965.
  Lyle E. Schaller, *Community Organization, Conflict, and Reconciliation* (Nashville: Abingdon Press, 1966).
  John Fish, *et al. The Edge of the Ghetto. A Study of Church Involvement in Community Organization,* 1966.
  Union Seminary Quarterly Review, January, 1967.
Church on the Mall in Philadelphia
  Presbyterian Life, November 15, 1967, pp. 8-11
Church of the Saviour in Washington, D.C.
  Elizabeth O'Connor, *Call to Commitment*
  ———. *Journey Inward, Journey Outward.* New York: Harper, 1968.
  Moore and Day, *Urban Church Breakthrough,* p. 34
  Time, June 13, 1967
  Union Seminary Quarterly Review, March, 1966, pp. 321-24
Coffeehouse Ministry
  Coffee Information Service, P.O. Box 2603, Grand Central Station, New York, N.Y. 10017
  "The Church Coffee House," distributed by the Department of Church Planning and Research with the Protestant Council of the City of New York (has an excellent bibliography)
  John D. Perry, *The Coffee House Ministry,* 1966
  The Methodist Story, June, 1966, p. 1
  Moore and Day, *Urban Church Breakthrough*
  Renewal magazine, May, 1965, p. 4
  Encounter magazine (Christian Theological Seminary), Autumn, 1966, pp. 317-22.
  Rose, ed. *Who's Killing the Church?* pp. 105-7.
East Harlem Protestant Parish in New York
  Bruce Kenrick. *Come out the Wilderness.*
  George W. Webber, *The Congregation in Mission* and *God's Colony in Man's World*
  Cities and Churches, ed. by Robert Lee, p. 162.
  Moore and Day, *Urban Church Breakthrough,* p. 133
Ecclesia Community in Rochester, New York
  Clark, *et al., The Church Creative,* pp. 61-71

Emmaus House in New York
  Newsweek, November 27, 1967, pp. 92-93
  New York Times, January 7, 1968, p. 1
Experimental Church in Winston-Salem, N.C.
  Christian Herald magazine, July, 1967, pp. 19-20, 65
First Congregational Church in Elmhurst, Ill.
  Renewal magazine, August, 1966, p. 23; and March, 1966, pp.
  6-8
First Methodist Church in Germantown, Pa.
  Robert Raines, *New Life in the Church*
  Renewal magazine, May, 1965, p. 10
  Clark, *et al., The Church Creative,* pp. 15-28
  Christian Century, October 27, 1965, pp. 1316-19
  Christian Advocate, September, 1963, pp. 9-10
  Rose, ed. *Who's Killing the Church?* pp. 70-76
Glide Memorial Church in San Francisco
  Together Magazine, April, 1965, p. 14
  Time, October 20, 1967, pp. 86-88
  The Wall Street Journal, March 13, 1967
Greater Urban Parish in Minneapolis
  Church in Metropolis magazine, November 8, 1966, p. 28
Industrial Mission
  Church in Metropolis magazine, Summer, 1966, pp. 26-29;
  and Spring, 1968, pp. 11-14
  Moore and Day, *Urban Church Breakthrough,* pp. 104 and 97
  Presbyterian Life, October 1, 1966, p. 6; and November 1,
  1966, p. 19
  Rose, ed. *Who's Killing the Church?* pp. 50-52
  Scott I. Paradise. *Detroit Industrial Mission.* New York:
  Harper, 1968.
Judson Memorial Church in New York
  Rose, ed. *Who's Killing the Church?* pp. 82-92
  Union Seminary Quarterly Review, March, 1966, pp. 328-33
  Kauffman, "Music by Al Carmines," *New York Times,* July
  3, 1966
  Kempton, "Beatitudes at Judson Memorial Church," *Esquire*
  magazine, March, 1966
Methodist Inner City Ministry in Atlanta
  World Outlook, November, 1965, pp. 32-33
Methodist Inner City Parish in Kansas City
  Together Magazine, May, 1966, pp. 50-56
  The Methodist Story, June, 1965, pp. 10-12
Metropolitan Associates of Philadelphia
  The Church for Others, pp. 74, 108-13
  United Church Herald, September, 1967, pp. 8-15

197

Church in Metropolis magazine, Fall, 1966, pp. 17-25
The Converted Church, pp. 105-10
Ministry to Leisure and Recreation
    National Council of Churches, *The Task Force on Leisure.* Report of the first meeting, October 24 and 25, 1965, in Princeton, N.J.
    Together Magazine, February, 1967
    The Lutheran, March 27, 1968, pp. 5-10
St. Augustine Episcopal Chapel in Washington, D.C.
    Grace Ann Goodman, *The Church and the Apartment House,* pp. 59-69
St. Clement's Episcopal Church in New York
    New York Times, October 31, 1965
    World Outlook magazine, September 19, 1966, and March, 1967, pp. 20-25
St. Marks' Church in the Bowery in New York
    Look, October 31, 1967, pp. 79-84
Trinity Temple Methodist Church in Louisville, Ky.
    Together magazine, February, 1964, p. 54
The Village Church in Milwaukee, Wis.
    The Lutheran, January 31, 1968, pp. 5-8
Wall Street Ministry
    Newsweek, October 30, 1967, p. 58
West St. Louis Ecumenical Parish
    Moore and Day, *Urban Church Breakthrough,* p. 143

INDEX

Page numbers in italics indicate that the reference is to a footnote.

Union Seminary Quarterly Review, 32, 125, 126
United Church Herald, 159
United Church of Christ, 23, 118, 148, 159, 177
Board of Homeland Ministries, 34, 154
Denominational Extension Dept., 42
United Methodist Church
Board of Missions, 19, 20
United Presbyterian Church in the USA, 23, 118, 143, 148
University of California (Berkeley), 80
University of Chicago, 162, 163
University of Michigan, 161
Urban Training Center (Chicago, Ill.), 19

Vahanian, Gabriel
Wait Without Idols, 187
Vail, Colo., 182, 183
Valley United Church of Christ (Concord, Calif.), 34-35, 41
Vietnam, 61, 62
Village Church (Milwaukee), 48-49

Wall Street Ministry (New York City), 146-50, 151, 155
Washington, D.C., 44, 49, 50, 51, 58, 68, 75, 88, 140, 141, 142, 143, 172, 188, 190
Webb, Pauline, *139*
Webber, George W., 19, 42, 62
The Congregation in Mission, 124
God's Colony in Man's World, 42, 124
Weber, Hans-Ruedi, 39

West, Charles (ed.)
The Missionary Church in East and West, 40
West Concord, Calif., 42
West St. Louis Ecumenical Parish (Mo.), 83-85, 190-91
Wieser, Thomas (ed.)
Planning for Mission, Working Papers on the New Quest for Missionary Communities, 42, 73, 76
Williams, Cecil, 79, 80
Williams, Colin W.
Where in the World? 17
Wilson, Charles E., Jr., 121
Winston-Salem, N.C., 46
Winter, Gibson, 81, 82, 107
The New Creation as Metropolis, 107
The Suburban Captivity of the Churches, 81
World, The, 96
World Council of Churches, 26, 39, 42, 66, 73
Western European Working Group, 42, 43, 72, 76
World Outlook, 97, 99
Wyon, Olive, 57

Ygnacio Valley, Calif., 42
Yokefellow Institute (Richmond, Ind.), 18
Yosemite Community Church (Calif.), 181-82
Yosemite National Park (Calif.), 181
Young, Lyle, 60, 61
Young Adult Center (San Francisco), 177
Young Adult Project (San Francisco), 177
Youth for Service (San Francisco), 79